The Rhetoric of Reaction

ALBERT O. HIRSCHMAN

The Rhetoric of Reaction

Perversity, Futility, Jeopardy

The Belknap Press of Harvard University Press

Cambridge, Massachusetts, and London, England 1991

This book is printed on acid-free paper, and its binding
materials have been chosen for strength and durability.

Library of Congress Cataloging-in-Publication Data

Hirschman, Albert O.
   The rhetoric of reaction : perversity, futility, jeopardy /
Albert O. Hirschman.
      p.   cm.
   Includes bibliographical references and index.
   ISBN 0-674-76867-1 (cloth).—ISBN 0-674-76868-X (paper)
   1. Conservatism—History. 2. Poor laws—History.
3. Suffrage—History. 4. Welfare state—History. I. Title.
JA83.H54   1991   90-2361
320.5′2′09—dc20   CIP

To Sarah,
my first reader and critic
for fifty years

Contents

Preface

"How does a person get to be that way?" In a *New Yorker* short story by Jamaica Kincaid (June 26, 1989, pp. 32–38), that question is asked repeatedly and insistently by a young woman from the Caribbean about her employer, Mariah—an effusive, excessively friendly, and somewhat obnoxious North American mother of four children. In the context, differences of social and racial background supply much of the answer. Yet, as I read the story, it struck me that Kincaid's question—a concern over the massive, stubborn, and exasperating otherness of others—is at the core of the present book.

The unsettling experience of being shut off, not just from the opinions, but from the entire life experience of large numbers of one's contemporaries is actually typical of modern democratic societies. In these days of universal celebration of the democratic model, it may seem churlish to dwell on deficiencies in the functioning of Western democracies. But it is precisely the spectacular and exhilarating crumbling of certain walls that calls attention to those that remain intact or to rifts that deepen. Among them there is one that can frequently be found in the more advanced democracies: the systematic lack of communication between groups of citizens, such as liberals

and conservatives, progressives and reactionaries. The resulting separateness of these large groups from one another seems more worrisome to me than the isolation of
anomic individuals in "mass society" of which sociologists
have made so much.

Curiously, the very stability and proper functioning of
a well-ordered democratic society depend on its citizens
arraying themselves in a few major (ideally two) clearly
defined groups holding different opinions on basic policy
issues. It can easily happen then that these groups become
walled off from each other—in this sense democracy con-
tinuously generates its own walls. As the process feeds on
itself, each group will at some point ask about the other,
in utter puzzlement and often with mutual revulsion,
"How did they get to be that way?"

In the mid-eighties, when this study was begun, that
was certainly how many liberals in the United States, including myself, looked at the ascendant and triumphant
conservative and neoconservative movement. One reaction to this state of affairs was to inquire into the conservative mind or personality. But this sort of head-on and
allegedly in-depth attack seemed unpromising to me: it
would widen the rift and lead, moreover, to an undue
fascination with a demonized adversary. Hence my deci-
sion to attempt a "cool" examination of surface phenomena: discourse, arguments, rhetoric, historically and ana-
lytically considered. In the process it would emerge that
discourse is shaped, not so much by fundamental personality traits, but simply by the *imperatives of argument,* almost
regardless of the desires, character, or convictions of the
participants. Exposing these servitudes might actually help

to loosen them and thus modify the discourse and restore communication.

That the procedure I have followed possesses such virtues is perhaps demonstrated by the way in which my analysis of "reactionary rhetoric" veers around, toward the end of the book, to encompass the liberal or progressive variety—somewhat to my own surprise.

The Rhetoric of Reaction

ONE

Two Hundred Years of Reactionary Rhetoric

In 1985, not long after the reelection of Ronald Reagan, the Ford Foundation launched an ambitious enterprise. Motivated no doubt by concern over mounting neoconservative critiques of social security and other social welfare programs, the Foundation decided to bring together a group of citizens who, after due deliberation and inspection of the best available research, would adopt an authoritative statement on the issues that were currently being discussed under the label "The Crisis of the Welfare State."[1]

In a magisterial opening statement, Ralf Dahrendorf (a member, like myself, of the group that had been assembled) placed the topic that was to be the subject of our discussions in its historical context by recalling a famous 1949 lecture by the English sociologist T. H. Marshall on the "development of citizenship" in the West.[2] Marshall had distinguished between the civil, political, and social dimensions of citizenship and then had proceeded to explain, very much in the spirit of the Whig interpretation of history, how the more enlightened human societies had successfully tackled one of these dimensions after the other. According to Marshall's scheme, which conveniently allocated about a century to each of the three tasks, the eighteenth century witnessed the major battles for the institution of *civil* citizenship—from freedom of speech, thought, and religion to the right to even-handed justice and other aspects of individual freedom or, roughly, the "Rights of Men" of the natural law doctrine and of the American and French Revolutions. In the course of the nineteenth century, it was the *political* aspect of citizenship, that is, the right of citizens to participate in the exercise of political power, that made major strides as the right to vote was extended to ever-larger groups. Finally, the rise of the Welfare State in the twentieth century extended the concept of citizenship to the *social and economic* sphere, by recognizing that minimal conditions of education, health, economic well-being, and security are basic to the life of a civilized being as well as to meaningful exercise of the civil and political attributes of citizenship.

When Marshall painted this magnificent and confident canvas of staged progress, the third battle for the assertion of citizenship rights, the one being waged on the social and economic terrain, seemed to be well on its way to being won, particularly in the Labour Party–ruled, social-security-conscious England of the immediate postwar period. Thirty-five years later, Dahrendorf could point out that Marshall had been overly optimistic on that score and that the notion of the socioeconomic dimension of citizenship as a natural and desirable complement of the civil and political dimensions had run into considerable difficulty and opposition and now stood in need of substantial rethinking.

Marshall's three-fold, three-century scheme conferred an august historical perspective on the group's task and provided an excellent jumping-off point for its deliberations. On reflection, however, it seemed to me that Dahrendorf had not gone far enough in his critique. Is it not true that not just the last but each and every one of Marshall's three progressive thrusts has been followed by ideological counterthrusts of extraordinary force? And have not these counterthrusts been at the origin of convulsive social and political struggles often leading to setbacks for the intended progressive programs as well as to much human suffering and misery? The backlash so far experienced by the Welfare State may in fact be rather mild in comparison with the earlier onslaughts and conflicts that followed upon the assertion of individual freedoms in the eighteenth century or upon the broadening of political participation in the nineteenth.

Once we contemplate this protracted and perilous seesawing of action and reaction, we come to appreciate more than ever the profound wisdom of Whitehead's wellknown observation, "The major advances in civilization are processes which all but wreck the societies in which they occur."[3] It is surely this statement rather than any account of smooth, unrelenting progress that catches the deeply ambivalent essence of the story so blandly entitled the "development of citizenship." Today one wonders in fact whether Whitehead, writing so somberly in the twenties, was perhaps too sanguine still: for some societies, and not the least, his sentence would be more nearly correct, so it could be argued, if the qualifying "all but" were omitted.

Three Reactions and Three Reactionary Theses

There are good reasons, then, for focusing on the reactions to the successive forward thrusts. To start with, I shall briefly state what I understand by the "three reactions," or reactionary waves, particularly since they may well be more diverse and diffuse than Marshall's fairly straightforward triad.

The first reaction is the movement of ideas following (and opposing) the assertion of equality before the law and of civil rights in general—Marshall's civil component of citizenship. There is a major difficulty in isolating this movement: the most resounding assertion of these rights occurred in the early stages and as a result of the French Revolution, so that the contemporary reaction against them was intertwined with opposition to the Revolution and all its works. To be sure, any opposition to the Declaration of the Rights of Man and the Citizen was motivated more by the events that led to the Declaration's being issued than by the text itself. But the radical counterrevolutionary discourse that soon emerged refused to distinguish between positive and negative aspects of the French Revolution—or to concede that there were any positive ones. Anticipating what was later to become a slogan of the Left *(la Révolution est un bloc),* the early adversaries of the Revolution considered it as a cohesive whole. Significantly, the first general indictment, Edmund Burke's *Reflections on the Revolution in France* (1790), started with a sustained polemic against the Declaration of the Rights of Man. Taking the ideology of the Revolution seriously, the counterrevolutionary discourse encompassed rejection of the text of which the revolutionaries were most proud. In this manner it became a fundamental intellectual current, laying the groundwork for much of the modern conservative position.

The second reactionary wave—the one opposing universal suffrage—was much less self-consciously counterrevolutionary or, in this juncture, counterreformist than the first. Few authors specifically proclaimed the objective of rolling back the advances of popular participation in politics that were achieved through extensions of the franchise (and by increasing the power of "lower" houses of parliament) in the course of the nineteenth century. In many countries the advance toward universal suffrage (only for men until the twentieth century) was a gradual affair, so that the critics found it difficult to take a unified stand. Moreover, there simply was no obvious stopping point for the forward march of political democracy once the traditional distinctions between nobility, clergy, and commoner had been obliterated. One can nevertheless *construct* an ideological countermovement from several influential currents that arose at about the time when the major breakthroughs in the struggle for extension of the franchise occurred. From the last third of the nineteenth century to the First World War and beyond, a vast and diffuse literature—embracing philosophy, psychology, politics, and belles lettres—amassed every conceivable argument for disparaging the "masses," the majority, parliamentary rule, and democratic government. Even though it made few proposals for alternative institutions, much of this literature implicitly or explicitly warned of the dire dangers threatening society as a result of the trend to democratization. With the benefit of hindsight, it is easy to hold such writings in part responsible for the destruction of democracy in Italy and Germany during the interwar period, and perhaps also for the antidemocratic turn taken by the Russian Revolution, as I shall argue at the end of Chapter 5. The second reaction may thus have to be given credit, if that is the correct term, for having produced history's most striking and disastrous instance of the self-fulfilling prophecy. Curiously, the reaction that was least consciously intent on reversing the ongoing trends or reforms became the one to have—or to be later accused of having had—the most destructive impact.

We are now coming to the third reactionary wave: the contemporary critique of the Welfare State and the attempts to roll back or "reform" some of its provisions. But these topics need not, perhaps, be reviewed at length here. As direct, day-to-day observers of this movement, we have a certain commonsense understanding of what is involved. At the same time, while a very large literature has by now criticized every aspect of the Welfare State from the economic and political points of view, and in spite of determined assaults upon social welfare programs and institutions by a variety of powerful political forces, it is too early to appraise the outcome of the new reactionary wave.

As will be apparent from this brief account, the size of my topic is enormous; in trying to get hold of it, I must be severely selective. It is therefore useful to point out right away what I am *not* attempting here. In the first place, I shall not write yet another volume on the nature and historic roots of conservative thought.[4] Rather, my aim is to delineate formal types of argument or rhetoric, and my emphasis will thus be on the major polemical postures and maneuvers likely to be engaged in by those who set out to debunk and overturn "progressive" policies and movements of ideas. Second, I am not going to embark on a broad and leisurely historical retelling of the successive reforms and counterreforms, theses and countertheses, since the French Revolution. Instead, I shall focus on a few common or typical arguments unfailingly made by each of the three reactive movements just noted. These arguments will constitute the basic subdivisions of my text. It is in conjunction with each argument that the "three reactions" will be drawn upon to ascertain the specific shape the argument has taken in various historical contexts.

Which are the arguments and how many are there? I must have an inbred urge toward symmetry. In canvassing for the principal ways of criticizing, assaulting, and ridiculing the three successive "progressive" thrusts of Marshall's story, I have come up with another triad: that is, with three principal reactive-reactionary theses, which I call the *perversity thesis* or thesis of the perverse effect, the *futility thesis,* and the *jeopardy thesis.* According to the *perversity* thesis, any purposive action to improve some feature of the political, social, or economic order only serves to exacerbate the condition one wishes to remedy. The *futility* thesis holds that attempts at social transformation will be unavailing, that they will simply fail to "make a dent." Finally, the *jeopardy* thesis argues that the cost of the proposed change or reform is too high as it endangers some previous, precious accomplishment.

These arguments are not, of course, the exclusive property of "reactionaries." They can be invoked by any group that opposes or criticizes new policy proposals or newly enacted policies. Whenever conservatives or reactionaries find themselves in power and are able to propose and carry out their own programs and policies, they may in their turn be attacked by liberals or progressives along the lines of the perversity, futility, and jeopardy theses. Nevertheless, the arguments are most typical of conservative attacks on existing or proposed progressive policies and their major protagonists have been conservative thinkers, as will be shown in Chapters 2 through 5. Chapter 6 deals with the corresponding arguments on the opposing progressive side; they are closely related to the reactionary theses, but take very different forms.

The next three, central chapters of this book deal with each of these theses in turn. Before I plunge into perversity, however, it will be helpful to review briefly the history of the terms "reaction" and "reactionary."

A Note on the Term "Reaction"

The couple "action" and "reaction" came into current usage as a result of Newton's third law of motion, which stated that "to every Action there is always opposed an equal Reaction."[5] Having thus been singled out for distinction in the then outstandingly prestigious science of mechanics, the two concepts spilled over to other realms and were widely used in the analysis of society and history in the eighteenth century. Montesquieu wrote, for example, "The parts of a state are related to one another like the parts of the universe: eternally linked together through the actions of some and the reactions of others."[6] Similarly, Newton's third law was specifically invoked by John Adams to justify a bicameral Congress, in the debate around the Constitution of the United States.[7]

No derogatory meaning whatsoever attached at first to the term "reaction." The remarkably durable infusion of this meaning took place during the French Revolution, specifically after its great watershed, the events of Thermidor.[8] It is already noticeable in Benjamin Constant's youthful tract *Des réactions politiques,* written in 1797 expressly to denounce what he perceived as a new chapter of the Revolution in which the reactions against the excesses of the Jacobins might themselves engender worse excesses. This very thought may have contributed to the derogatory meaning that arose, but Constant's text supplies a further hint. Somewhat surprisingly, the next-to-last sentence of his pamphlet is an unreconstructed paean to progress: "Ever since the spirit of man has undertaken its forward march . . . no invasion of barbarians, no coalition of oppressors, and no invocation of prejudices are able to make him move back."[9]

The spirit of the Enlightenment, with its belief in the forward march of history, had apparently survived the Revolution, even among its critics, notwithstanding the Terror and other mishaps. One could deplore the "excesses" of the Revolution, as Constant certainly did, yet continue to believe both in history's fundamentally progressive design and in the Revolution's being part of it. Such must have been the dominant contemporary attitude. Otherwise it would be hard to explain why those who "reacted" to the Revolution in a predominantly negative manner came to be perceived and denounced as "reactionaries," who wanted "to turn the clock back." Here, incidentally, is another term showing how much our language is under the influence of the belief in progress: it implies that the mere unraveling of time brings human improvement, so that any return to an earlier period would be calamitous.

From the point of view of my inquiry, the negative implication of the terms "reaction" and "reactionary" is unfortunate, as I would like to be able to use them without constantly injecting a value judgment. For this reason I resort on occasion to alternative, more neutral terms such as "counterthrust," "reactive," and so on. Most of the time, however, I adhere to the more common usage, occasionally employing quotation marks to signal that I do not mean to write in a vituperative mode.

The Perversity Thesis

Exploring the semantics of the term "reaction" points straight to an important characteristic of "reactionary" thinking. Because of the stubbornly progressive temper of the modern era, "reactionaries" live in a hostile world. They are up against an intellectual climate in which a positive value attaches to whatever lofty objective is placed on the social agenda by self-proclaimed "progressives." Given this state of public opinion, reactionaries are not likely to launch an all-out attack on that objective. Rather, they will endorse it, sincerely or otherwise, but then attempt to demonstrate that the action proposed or undertaken is ill conceived; indeed, they will most typically urge that this action will produce, via a chain of unintended consequences, the *exact contrary* of the objective being proclaimed and pursued.

This is, at first blush, a daring intellectual maneuver. The structure of the argument is admirably simple, whereas the claim being made is rather extreme. It is not just asserted that a movement or a policy will fall short of its goal or will occasion unexpected costs or negative side effects: rather, so goes the argument, *the attempt to push society in a certain direction will result in its moving all right, but in the opposite direction.* Simple, intriguing, and devastating (if true), the argument has proven popular with generations of "reactionaries" as well as fairly effective with the public at large. In current debates it is often invoked as the counterintuitive, counterproductive, or, most to the point, *perverse* effect of some "progressive" or "well-intentioned" public policy.[1] Attempts to reach for liberty will make society sink into slavery, the quest for democracy will produce oligarchy and tyranny, and social welfare programs will create more, rather than less, poverty. *Everything backfires.*

The French Revolution and Proclamation of the Perverse Effect

Like many other key elements of reactionary rhetoric, this argument was proclaimed as a cardinal principle in the wake of the French Revolution and can be found already in Edmund Burke's *Reflections on the Revolution in France.* Actually, there was little need for inventive genius: as Liberté, Egalité, Fraternité turned into the dictatorship of the Comité de Salut Public (and later into that of Bonaparte), the thought that certain attempts to reach for liberty are bound to lead to tyranny instead almost forced itself upon one's mind. It is, moreover, an ancient observation and argument that democracy easily degenerates into tyranny. What was remarkable about Burke's writings was, first of all, that he predicted such an outcome as early as 1790, and, second, that his scattered remarks on the topic were soon turned into an allegedly fundamental insight into social dynamics. Burke prognosticated that "an ignoble oligarchy, founded on the destruction of the crown, the church, the nobility, and the people [would] end all the deceitful dreams and visions of the equality and the rights of men." Also, he conjured up the spectacle of military interventions during various civil disorders and exclaimed, "Massacre, torture, hanging! These are your rights of men!"[2]

The English historian Alfred Cobban commented that Burke's "accurate prediction of the course the Revolution would take . . . is a vindication of the virtue of just theory."[3] Whatever "just" or correct theory did lie behind Burke's analysis, many of his contemporaries were impressed, not merely by the force of his eloquence but by the surety of his vision. The argument took root and was to be repeated and generalized, particularly by foreign observers who were trying to draw practical "lessons" for their countries from what was happening or had happened in France. Thus Schiller wrote in 1793:

> The attempt of the French people to install the holy Rights of Man and to conquer political liberty has only brought to light its impotence and unworthiness in this regard; the result has been that not just this unhappy people, but alongside it a considerable part of Europe and a whole century have been thrown back into barbarism and servitude.[4]

A particularly sweeping, if heavy-footed, formulation is that of the German romantic political economist Adam Müller, a close friend and protégé of Friedrich von Gentz, the aide of Metternich who as a young man had translated Burke's *Reflections* into German. When the Revolution and its Napoleonic aftermath had run their course, Müller proclaimed:

> The history of the French Revolution constitutes a proof, administered continuously over thirty years, that man, acting by himself and without religion, is unable to break any chains that oppress him without sinking in the process into still deeper slavery.[5]

Here Burke's conjectures have been turned into a rigid historical law that could serve as an ideological prop for the Europe of the Holy Alliance.

Burke's uncanny ability to project the course of the French Revolution has been attributed to the very strength of his passionate engagement with it.[6] But it may be suggested that his formulation of the perverse effect has an intellectual origin as well: he was steeped in the thought of the Scottish Enlightenment, which had stressed the importance of the unintended effects of human action. The best-known application of this notion was the Invisible Hand doctrine of Adam Smith, with whose economic views Burke had expressed total agreement.

Smith, like Mandeville and others (such as Pascal and Vico) before him, had shown how individual actions motivated by greed and the desire for luxury (Mandeville's "private vices")—or, less insultingly, by self-interest—can have a positive social outcome in the shape of a more prosperous commonwealth. Expressing these ideas with poetic pith toward the end of the century, Goethe defined his Mephisto as "a part of that force that ever wills evil, but ever brings forth good."

In this manner the intellectual terrain was well prepared for arguing that on occasion the opposite might happen. This was exactly what Burke did when he was faced with the unprecedented enterprise of the French Revolution to reconstruct society: he made good and evil switch places in Mephisto's statement and asserted that the social outcome of the revolutionaries' striving for the public good would be evil, calamitous, and wholly contrary to the goals and hopes they were professing.

From one point of view, then, Burke's proposition looks (and may have looked to him) like a minor variation on a well-known eighteenth-century theme. From another, it was a radical ideological shift from the Enlightenment to romanticism and from optimism about progress to pessimism. Large-scale and seemingly abrupt ideological shifts may take place in precisely this fashion. Formally they require only a slight modification of familiar patterns of thought, but the new variant has an affinity for very different beliefs and propositions and becomes *embedded* in them to form a wholly new gestalt, so that in the end the intimate connection between the old and the new is almost unrecognizable.

In the present case the starting point for this kind of transformation was the slow emergence of a new hope for world order. From the sixteenth century on it was widely agreed that religious precept and moral admonition could not be relied on to restrain and reshape human nature so as to guarantee social order and economic welfare. With the rise of commerce and industry in the seventeenth and eighteenth centuries, influential voices proposed that some of the ineradicable "vices" of men, such as persistent self-seeking, could, properly channeled, produce a minimally workable and perhaps even a progressive society. To Pascal, Vico, and Goethe this paradoxical process suggested the intervention of a Providence that is remarkably *benign,* forgiving, and helpful as it transmutes evil into

15

good. The optimistic message of this construction was enhanced further when the pursuit of self-interest through trade and industry lost its stigma and was accorded social prestige instead. Perhaps this development came about as the result of some inevitable contamination of the means by the end. If the outcome of some process is odious, it is difficult, in the longer run, to maintain that the motives and activities leading up to it are wholly commendable. The opposite is also true: when the outcome is benign, this is bound to reflect eventually on the underlying activities. But once there is no longer a sharp contrast between the means and the end, or between process and outcome, the need for the magical intervention of Divine Providence becomes less compelling—Adam Smith in fact barely allowed it to survive, secularized and a bit anemic, as the Invisible Hand.* In other words, to the eighteenth-century mind society was left standing erect and functioning nicely even though the support of God was being gradually withdrawn from it—a vision of the social universe without God far less tragic, we may note in passing, than the one that was to be entertained a century later by Dostoevsky and Nietzsche.

The thinking about unintended outcomes of human action received a new impulse with the events of the

---

*In his 1966 lectures on *The Role of Providence in the Social Order* (Philadelphia: American Philosophical Society, 1972), and particularly in the third lecture, "The Invisible Hand and Economic Man," Jacob Viner demonstrated the continued hold that teleological thought had on Adam Smith. It is significant, nevertheless, that Smith introduced the secular concept "Invisible Hand" as a substitute for the Divine Providence which had been routinely invoked in most earlier writings expressing a teleological view of order in nature and society.

French Revolution. As the strivings for liberty ended in terror and tyranny, the critics of the Revolution perceived a new and striking disparity between individual intentions and social outcomes. Divine Providence was pressed back into active service, but in a shape that was anything but benign: her task now was to *foil* the designs of men, whose pretensions to build an ideal society were to be exposed as naive and preposterous, if not as criminal and blasphemous. *Der Mensch in seinem Wahn* (Man in his delusion), that "most terrible of terrors," as Schiller put it in one of his best-known as well as surprisingly conservative poems *(Das Lied von der Glocke)*, had to be taught a salutary if severe lesson.

Joseph de Maistre in particular endows the Divine Providence he sees at work throughout the Revolution with refined cruelty. In his *Considérations sur la France* (1797) he regards it as providential for the Revolution to have generated its own lengthy internecine conflicts; for, he argues, if there had been an early successful counterrevolution, the revolutionaries would have had to be tried in official courts and then one of two things would have happened: either the verdicts would have been considered excessive by public opinion or, more likely, they would have fallen far short of full justice in being limited to just a few great criminals *(quelques grands coupables)*. Maistre then proclaims, "This is precisely what Providence did not want," and why she cleverly arranged matters in such a way that much larger numbers of guilty were made to "fall under the blows of their own accomplices."*

---

*Considérations sur la France, ed. Jean-Louis Darcel (Geneva: Slatkine, 1980), pp. 74–75. The extent to which Maistre carried his bizarre

Finally, almost at the end of his book, Maistre comes forward with an extravagant formulation of the perversity thesis as the very essence of Divine Providence. In speculating how the confidently expected counterrevolution and restoration of the Monarchy will actually come about, he first declares that the "multitude . . . never obtains what it wishes" and then pushes this thought to the limit:

> One can even note an *affectation* (may I be permitted to use this expression) of Providence: the efforts people make to attain a certain objective are precisely the means employed by Providence to keep it out of reach . . . If one wants to know the probable result of the French Revolution, one only needs to examine the points on which all factions were in agreement: all wanted the . . . destruction of universal Christianity and of the Monarchy; *from which it follows* that the final result of their efforts will be none other than the exaltation of Christianity and Monarchy.

All those who have written or meditated about history have admired this secret force which mocks human intentions.*

---

speculations must on reflection have appeared excessive even to him, for he eliminated the following related passage from his definitive text: "[Divine Providence] passes its sentences and the guilty who are slain by killing one another do nothing but carry them out. Perhaps she will set aside one or another for human justice but when the latter will resume its rights, at least it will not be encumbered by the large number of guilty" (p.75n). [Unless otherwise noted, passages given in translation throughout this book were rendered by the author.]

*Ibid., pp. 156–157. Emphasis in original. Through the various emphases and the parenthetical clause Maistre reveals his excitement

One could not wish for a more extreme statement. Maistre's total conviction about Providence's unfailingly arranging for an outcome of human actions that is the precise opposite of human intentions reminds one of certain parents who, having observed the contrary behavior of their child, hit on the idea of telling the child to do the exact opposite of what they want him or her to do. Most parents soon realize, of course, that the idea is less bright than it seemed at first.

Maistre's construction of Divine Providence is no doubt exceptional in its elaborate vengefulness and in its seamless invocation of the perverse effect. But the basic feature of the perversity thesis has remained unchanged: man is held up to ridicule—by Divine Providence and by those privileged social analysts who have pierced her designs—for in setting out to improve the world radically, he goes radically astray. What better way to show him up as half foolish and half criminal than to prove that he is achieving the exact opposite of what he is proclaiming as his objective? What better argument, moreover, against a policy one abhors, but whose announced aim one does not care to attack head-on?

Universal Suffrage and Its Alleged Perverse Effects

Hence the identical line of reasoning surfaces again during our next episode, the broadening of the franchise in

---

about having a deep and daring insight here. For the close connection of Maistre's train of thought to one aspect of the Oedipus myth, see Chapter 4.

the course of the nineteenth century. New reasons for affirming the inevitability of a perverse outcome of that process were now put forward by the emergent social sciences. For an appreciation of the climate of opinion in which these arguments arose, it is useful to be aware of contemporary attitudes toward the masses and toward mass participation in politics.

Because of the frequent outbursts of civil strife of one kind or another in recent history, it is widely assumed that a close relation exists between such outbursts and the strength with which conflicting beliefs are held by opposing groups of the citizenry. Since a long, bloody civil war was fought in the United States over the slavery issue, everyone is convinced that the division of opinion over that issue was sharp and deep. Inversely, inasmuch as the extension of the franchise in Western Europe in the course of the nineteenth century was achieved in a fairly gradual and peaceful manner, the temptation is to think that opposition to that process was not particularly strenuous. Nothing could be farther from the truth. After all, Europe had long been a highly stratified society with the lower classes being held in the utmost contempt by both the upper and the middle classes. It must be recalled, for example, that an enlightened and not particularly aristocratic person like Burke wrote, in the *Reflections:* "The occupation of a hairdresser, or of a working tallow chandler cannot be a matter of honor to any person . . . to say nothing of a number of other more servile employments . . . The state suffers oppression if such as they . . . are permitted to rule." Later he comments in passing on the "innumerable servile, degrading, unseemly, unmanly, and often most unwholesome and pestiferous occupations to which by the social economy so many wretches are inevitably doomed."[7]

Such remarks, made in an offhand manner, suggest that Burke's primary emotion toward the "lower orders" was not so much class antagonism and fear of revolt as utter contempt and feelings of total separateness, even of outright physical revulsion, much as in caste societies. This mood carried over into the nineteenth century and could only have been enhanced by the cityward migration of impoverished rural folk that came with industrialization. Shortly it was compounded with fear as Burke's "wretches" took to staging violent political outbreaks, particularly in the 1840s. After one such episode in 1845 in nearby Lucerne, the young Jacob Burckhardt wrote from Basel:

> Conditions in Switzerland—so disgusting and barbarous—have spoilt everything for me and I shall expatriate myself as soon as I can . . . The word freedom sounds rich and beautiful, but no one should talk about it who has not seen and experienced slavery under the loud-mouthed masses, called the "people," seen it with his own eyes, and endured civil unrest . . . I know too much history to expect anything from the despotism of the masses but a future tyranny, which will mean the end of history.[8]

It would be easy to collect additional evidence on the extent to which the idea of mass participation in politics, even though in the watered-down form of universal suffrage, must have seemed aberrant and potentially disastrous to a good part of Europe's elites. Universal suffrage was one of Flaubert's favorite bêtes noires, a frequent butt

for his passionate hatred of human stupidity. With heavy
irony, universal suffrage figures in his *Dictionnaire des idées
reçues* as the "last word of political science." In his letters
he pronounced it "the shame of the human spirit" and
the equal of (or worse than) other absurd notions, such as
the divine right of kings or the infallibility of the pope.
The basis of these judgments was the conviction that the
"people," the "mass," is always stupid *(idiot)*, inept, "under
age."[9] In general, Flaubert reserved his greatest scorn for
the *bêtise* of the bourgeoisie, but, being generous in his
dislikes, he had no problem manifesting similarly negative
feelings toward the masses; at one point he even achieved
consistency between these attitudes as he wrote mockingly
about "the dream [of some] to raise the proletariat to the
level of stupidity of the bourgeoisie."[10]

Elsewhere in Europe similar feelings prevailed. The
more universal suffrage extended its sweep across Europe,
the more strident became the elite voices that stood or
arose in unreconciled opposition to it. For Nietzsche, popular elections were the ultimate expression of the "herd
instinct," a telling term he coined to denigrate all trends
toward democratic politics. Even Ibsen, acclaimed in his
time as a progressive critic of society, harshly attacked the
majority and majority rule. In *An Enemy of the People* (1882)
the play's hero (Dr. Stockmann) thunders:

> Who forms the majority in any country? I think we'd
> all have to agree that the fools are in a terrifying,
> overwhelming majority all over the world! But in the
> name of God it can't be right that the fools should
> rule the wise! . . . The majority has the power, unfor-
> tunately . . . but the majority is not right! The ones

who are right are a few isolated individuals like me! The minority is always right![11]

Here is an interesting point of intersection-collision of two lines of thought, both originating in the eighteenth century: the demand for political democracy, on the one hand, with equal rights for all citizens, and, on the other, the existence and special, privileged status of a "few isolated individuals." Ibsen evidently points here to the *genius*, another concept first fully elaborated during the Enlightenment, at the hands of Diderot, Helvétius, and others.[12]

So much for the climate of opinion around T. H. Marshall's second progressive wave, the advent of political equality via the franchise. In contrast to the idea of free trade, this particular embodiment of "progress" never achieved anything like ideological hegemony, not even for as much as a decade or two—at least in the nineteenth century. To the contrary, the undoubted advance of democratic political forms in the second half of the century took place in the midst of a diffuse mood of skepticism and hostility. Then, toward the century's end, this mood found a more sophisticated expression in social scientific theories, as medical and psychological discoveries showed human behavior to be motivated by irrational forces to a much greater extent than had been acknowledged before. The idea of basing political governance on universal suffrage could henceforth be exposed as a belated product and, indeed, as an obsolete relic of the Enlightenment with its abiding belief in rationality. This belief would now be exposed not just as "shallow," the standard Romantic critique, but as plain wrong.

Among the several political ideas that can be considered to be, in this manner, reactions to the advances of the franchise and of democracy in general, one of the more prominent and influential was articulated by Gustave Le Bon in his best-selling *Psychologie des foules,* first published in 1895. It exemplifies once again the attraction of reactionary thinkers to the perverse effect.

Le Bon's principal argument challenges commonsense understandings in the manner of what is known to economists as the *fallacy of composition:* a proposition that applies to the individual does not necessarily hold for the group, much less for the crowd. Impressed by recent medical-research findings on infection, contamination, and hypnosis, and unaware of the simultaneously proceeding work of Freud that would shortly show individuals themselves to be subject to all manner of unconscious drives, Le Bon based his theory on a sharp dichotomy between the individual and the crowd: the individual is rational, perhaps sophisticated and calculating; the crowd is irrational, easily swayed, unable to weigh pros and cons, given to unreasoning enthusiasms, and so on.* Even though occasionally the crowd is accorded some good points because of its ability to engage in acts of selfless abnegation (soldiers in battle), there is no doubt that Le Bon looks at the crowd as a lower, though dangerously vigorous, form

---

*Oddly, when Freud turned to the problem of mass psychology after World War I he did not remark on what, from the point of view of his own theory, was surely a much overdrawn distinction between the individual and the crowd on the part of Le Bon. See his generally appreciative comments on Le Bon and *Psychologie des foules* in *Group Psychology and the Analysis of the Ego* (1921), in Freud, *Works* (London: Hogarth, 1955), vol. 18, pp. 72–81.

of life: "None too good at reasoning, the crowd is on the contrary much given to action."[13] This action takes typically the form either of anomic outbreaks by "criminal crowds" or of enthusiastic, hypnotic mass movements organized by demagogic leaders (*meneurs*, not *chefs*) who know how to enslave the crowd according to a few simple rules obligingly supplied by Le Bon.

In fin-de-siècle Europe, Le Bon's theory had obvious political implications. It saw the prospects for national and international order as quite gloomy: with the franchise spreading, Le Bon's irrational crowds were installed as important actors in an ever-larger number of countries. Moreover, the book's last two chapters, "Electoral Crowds" and "Parliamentary Assemblies," supply specific arguments against modern mass-based democracy. Here Le Bon does not argue directly against universal suffrage; rather, like Flaubert, he speaks of it as an absurd dogma which is unfortunately bound to cause a great deal of harm, just as did earlier superstitious beliefs. "Only time can act on them," he writes, assuming the stance of a resigned chronicler of human folly. Nor does Le Bon propose to improve the system by returning to restrictions on the right to vote. His basic principle being that the crowd is always benighted, he makes it apply with remarkable consistency, regardless of the constituents of the crowd and of their characteristics as individuals: "the vote of 40 academicians is no better than that of 40 water carriers" he wrote, thereby managing to insult in passing the French Academy with its forty members, an elite body from which he resentfully felt himself excluded.[14]

This nonreformist position permits Le Bon to outline coldly the disastrous consequences of universal suffrage:

anticipating our contemporary "public choice" theorists, he first demonstrates how parliamentary democracy fosters a tendency toward ever more public spending, in response to the pressure of sectional interests. The perverse effect is appealed to in the final, crowning argument of the book: vaunted democracy will increasingly turn into the rule of bureaucracy through the many laws and regulations that are being passed in "the illusion that equality and liberty will be better safeguarded thereby."[15] In support of these views, he cites *The Man versus the State* (1884), a collection of Herbert Spencer's late essays. Here was a contemporary scientific authority figure who had taken a strongly conservative turn. Spencer too had chosen the perverse effect as his leitmotif, particularly in the essay entitled "The Sins of Legislators," where he put forward an extravagantly general formulation: "uninstructed legislators have in past times continually increased human suffering in their endeavours to mitigate it."[16]

Once again, then, a group of social analysts found itself irresistibly attracted to deriding those who aspire to change the world for the better. And it is not enough to show that these naive *Weltverbesserer* fall flat on their faces: it must be proven that they are actually, if I may coin the corresponding German term, *Weltverschlechterer* (world worseners), that they leave the world in a worse shape than prevailed before any "reform" had been instituted.* Moreover, the worsening must be shown to occur along

---

*The term *Weltverbesserer* has a derisive meaning in German, probably as a result of the particularly strong German reaction against what came to be routinely denounced as the "shallow" Enlightenment *(seichte Aufklärung)*.

the very dimension where there was supposed to be improvement.

The Poor Laws and the Welfare State

This sort of argument was to achieve special prominence during the third reactionary phase, to which I now turn: the present-day assault on the economic and social policies that make up the modern Welfare State.

In economics, more than in the other social and political sciences, the perverse-effect doctrine is closely tied to a central tenet of the discipline: the idea of a self-regulating market. To the extent that this idea is dominant, any public policy aiming to change market outcomes, such as prices or wages, automatically becomes noxious interference with beneficent equilibrating processes. Even economists who are favorable to some measures of income and wealth redistribution tend to regard the most obvious "populist" measures of that sort as counterproductive.

The perverse effect of specific interferences has often been argued by tracing demand and supply reactions to such measures. As a result of, say, a price stop for bread, it is shown how flour will be diverted to other final uses and how some bread will be sold at black-market prices, so that the average price of bread may go up rather than down as was intended. Similarly, when a minimum wage is established or raised, it is easy to show how employment is likely to drop, so that the aggregate income of the workers may fall rather than rise. As Milton Friedman puts it with his usual superb assurance, "Minimum wage laws are about as clear a case as one can find of a measure the effects of which are precisely the opposite of those intended by the men of good will who support it."[17]

There is actually nothing certain about these perverse effects, particularly in the case of so basic an economic parameter as the wage. Once a minimum wage is introduced, the underlying demand and supply curves for labor could shift; moreover, the officially imposed rise in remunerations could have a positive effect on labor productivity and consequently on employment. An expectation of such effects is indeed the principal rationale for the establishment of a realistic minimum wage. More as a result of the implicit moral suasion and establishment of a public standard of fairness than through the threat of penalties, the proclamation of a minimum wage can have a real effect on the conditions at which workers offer their labor and employers bid for it. But the undoubted possibility of a perverse outcome makes for an excellent debating point which is bound to be brought up in any polemic.

The long discussion about problems of social assistance to the poor provides ample illustration for these various arguments. Such assistance is admittedly and often self-consciously rank interference with "market outcomes" that assign some members of society to the low end of the income scale. The economic argument on the ensuing perverse effects was first put forward during the debates about the Poor Laws in England. The critics of these laws, from Defoe to Burke and from Malthus to Tocqueville, scoffed at the notion that the Poor Laws were merely a "safety net," to use a current term, for those who had fallen behind, through no fault of their own, in the race for a livelihood. Given the human "proclivity to idleness" (to use Mandeville's phrase), this "naive" view neglected the supply reactions, the incentives built into the arrangement: the availability of the assistance, so it was argued, acts as a positive encouragement to "sloth" and "depravity" and thus *produces* poverty instead of relieving it. Here is a typical formulation of this point by an early-nineteenth-century English essayist:

> The Poor-laws were intended to prevent mendicants; they have made mendicancy a legal profession; they were established in the spirit of a noble and sublime provision, which contained all the theory of Virtue; they have produced all the consequences of Vice . . . The Poor-laws, formed to relieve the distressed, have been the arch-creator of distress.[18]

A century and a half later, one reads in the most highly publicized attack on the Welfare State in the United States, Charles Murray's *Losing Ground* (1984):

> We tried to provide more for the poor and produced more poor instead. We tried to remove the barriers to escape from poverty and inadvertently built a trap.[19]

Except for a slight toning down of nineteenth-century coloratura, the melody is exactly the same. The perverse effect would seem to work unremittingly under both early and late capitalism.

Not that the ideological scene has remained unchanged throughout these 150 years. The success of Murray's book in fact owes much to the rather fresh look of its principal point, epitomized in its title—almost any idea that has not been around for a while stands a good chance of being mistaken for an original insight. What actually has happened is that the idea went into hiding, for reasons that are of some interest to our story.

As Karl Polanyi showed memorably in *The Great Transformation* (1944), the English Poor Laws, especially as supplemented and reinforced by the Speenhamland Act of 1795, represented a last-ditch attempt to rein in, through public assistance, the free market for labor and its effects on the poorest strata of society. By supplementing low wages, particularly in agriculture, the new scheme was helpful in ensuring social peace and in sustaining domestic food production during the age of the Napoleonic Wars.

But once the emergency was over, the accumulating drawbacks of the system of combining relief and wages came under strong attack. Supported by belief in the new political economy "laws" of Bentham, Malthus, and Ricardo, the reaction against the Speenhamland Act became so strong that in 1834 the Poor Law Amendment Act (or "New Poor Law") fashioned the workhouse into the exclusive instrument of social assistance. In response to critics of the more generous earlier system, workhouse assistance was now organized so as to do away once and for all with any conceivable perverse effect. To this end, the new arrangements were meant to deter the poor from resorting to public assistance and to stigmatize those who did by "imprisoning [them] in workhouses, compelling them to wear special garb, separating them from their families, cutting them off from communication with the poor outside and, when they died, permitting their bodies to be disposed of for dissection."[20]

It was not long before this new regime aroused in turn

violent criticism. As early as 1837 Disraeli inveighed against it in his election campaign: "I consider that this Act has disgraced the country more than any other upon record. Both a moral crime and a political blunder, it announces to the world that in England poverty is a crime."[21]

Critics of the law came from a wide spectrum of opinion and social groups. A particularly powerful and influential indictment was Dickens' novel *Oliver Twist,* published in 1837–38. A strong anti–Poor Law movement arose, complete with demonstrations and riots, during the decade following enactment; as a result, the provisions of the law were not fully applied, especially in the north, the center of both the opposition and the textile industry.[22] It became uncomfortably clear that there were many evils—loss of community, forgoing of common decency, and internal strife—that could be worse than the alleged "promotion of idleness" whose elimination had been so singlemindedly pursued by the 1834 statute. In E. P. Thompson's retrospective judgment, "the Act of 1834 . . . was perhaps the most sustained attempt to impose an ideological dogma, in defiance of the evidence of human needs, in English history."[23]

The experience with the New Poor Law was so searing that the argument which had presided over its adoption—essentially the perverse effect of social welfare assistance—remained discredited for a long time. This may in fact be one reason for the rather smooth, if slow, emergence of welfare-state legislation in England during the late nineteenth and early twentieth centuries.

Eventually the argument reappeared, notably in the United States. But even in this country it was not put forward at first in its crude form, as in the statement already cited from Murray's *Losing Ground*. Rather, it looks as though to be reintroduced into polite company the old-fashioned perverse effect needed some special, sophisticated attire. Thus, one of the early general attacks on social welfare policy in this country had the intriguing title "Counterintuitive Behavior of Social Systems."[24] Written by Jay W. Forrester, a pioneer in the simulation of social processes by computer models and an adviser to a then-influential international group of notables known as the Club of Rome, the article is a good example of what the French call intellectual terrorism. At the outset the readers are told that they have a very poor chance of understanding how society works, since we are dealing with "complex and highly interacting systems," with social arrangements that "belong to the class called multi-loop nonlinear feedback systems" and similar arcane "system dynamics" that "the human mind is not adapted to interpreting." Only the highly trained computer specialist can unravel these mysteries. And what revelations does Forrester come up with? "At times programs cause exactly the reverse of desired results"! For example, most urban policies, from job creation to low-cost housing, "range from ineffective to harmful judged either by their effect on the economic health of the city or by their long-range effect on the low-income population." In other words, Joseph de Maistre's vengeful Divine Providence has returned to the stage in the guise of Forrester's "feedback-loop dynamics," and the result is identical: any human attempt to improve society only makes matters worse.

Stripped of its hi-tech language, the article simply reflects the widespread disappointment that followed upon

Lyndon Johnson's Great Society. As often happens, the exaggerated promises of that program led to similarly exaggerated assertions of *total failure,* an intellectual stance I first described at length in a book on policy-making in Latin America.*

In an influential article, also written in 1971, entitled "The Limits of Social Policy," Nathan Glazer joined Forrester in invoking the perverse effect. The article starts ominously, "There is a general sense that we face a crisis in social policy," and wastes little time before proclaiming,

---

*In *Journeys Toward Progress* (New York: Twentieth Century Fund, 1963) I studied three protracted policy problems in three Latin American countries. One of them was the process of land-tenure reform in Colombia; an important episode of that process was a land reform law ("Law 200") of 1936 which was aimed at turning tenants into owners and at improving the conditions of rural dwellers in various other ways. According to most local accounts, the effects of the reform were wholly perverse: the passage of the law caused landowners to eject their tenants from lands they had rented, thereby converting them into landless laborers. I became suspicious of the automatic, knee-jerk way in which such assertions of perversity peppered historical accounts, newspaper articles, and political speeches of both conservative and "radical" writers. Upon researching the historical record, I became convinced that Law 200 had been unjustly defamed and that it had a variety of useful accomplishments to its credit (see *Journeys,* pp. 107–113). It turns out that I battled the excessive claims of the perversity thesis many years ago.

This and similar experiences with the way public policy is assimilated and history written in Latin America made me suggest that policy analysis and historiography are strongly imprinted there with some deep-set "failure complex," and I later coined and repeatedly used the term "fracasomania" to denote the trait. I now realize that this cultural interpretation was too narrow. Arguing along the lines of the perversity thesis, as was done so insistently by the Colombian commentators on Law 200, appears to have many attractions for parties who are not necessarily affected by fracasomania.

in quite general terms, "Our efforts to deal with distress themselves increase distress."[25]

In arguing for this dispiriting conclusion, Glazer did not appeal to computer models but spelled out instead some plain sociological reasons. Welfare-state policies, he argued, are meant to deal with distress that used to be taken care of by traditional structures such as the family, the church, or the local community. As these structures break down, the state comes in to take over their functions. In the process the state causes further weakening of what remains of the traditional structures. Hence there arises a greater need for public assistance than was anticipated and the situation gets worse rather than better.

Rather narrow limits are set to the damage that can be caused by the perverse effect as formulated by Glazer. It all depends on what remains of the traditional structures at the time the welfare state arrives on the scene, as well as on the accuracy of the assumption that these residues will then promptly disintegrate so as to throw a greater-than-expected burden on the state. One wonders whether there is really no way in which the two sources of assistance can ever be made to coexist and perhaps to complement each other.[26]

In any event, Glazer's reasoning was too softly "sociological" for the harder conservative mood that became fashionable during the eighties. Charles Murray's formulation of the perverse effect of social welfare policy returned to the blunt reasoning of the proponents of Poor Law reform in early-nineteenth-century England. Inspired, like them, by the simplest economic verities, he argued that public assistance to the poor, as available in the United States, acts as an irresistible incentive to those working or potentially working at low wages or salaries (his famous "Harold" and "Phyllis") to flock to the welfare rolls and to stay there—to become forever "trapped" in sloth and poverty. If this were true, the perverse "poverty-creating" effect of poor relief in the United States would of course assume huge and disastrous proportions.

Reflections on the Perversity Thesis

Just as earlier I have not controverted Burke or Le Bon, it is not my purpose here to discuss the substance of the various arguments against social welfare policies in the United States and elsewhere. What I have tried to show is how the protagonists of this "reactionary" episode, just as those of the earlier ones, have been powerfully attracted time and again by the same form of reasoning, that is, the claim of the perverse effect. I must apologize for the monotony of my account—but it was deliberate, for in it lies the demonstration of my point that invocation of the perversity thesis is a basic characteristic of reactionary rhetoric. This reiteration of the argument may have had the unfortunate effect of conveying the impression that situations exhibiting perversity are in fact ubiquitous. Actually, my intention is to put forward two propositions of equal weight: (1) the perverse effect is widely appealed to by reactionary thought, *and* (2) it is unlikely to exist "out there" to anything like the extent that is claimed. I shall now speak, much more briefly, to the second proposition.

One of the great insights of the science of society—found already in Vico and Mandeville and elaborated magisterially during the Scottish Enlightenment—is the observation that, because of imperfect foresight, human actions are apt to have unintended consequences of considerable scope. Reconnaissance and systematic description of such unintended consequences have ever since been a major assignment, if not the raison d'être, of social science.

The perverse effect is a special and extreme case of the unintended consequence. Here the failure of foresight of ordinary human actors is well-nigh total as their actions are shown to produce precisely the opposite of what was intended; the social scientists analyzing the perverse effect, on the other hand, experience a great feeling of superiority—and revel in it. Maistre naively said as much when he exclaimed in his gruesome chapter on the prevalence of war in human history: "It is sweet [*doux*] to fathom the design of the Godhead in the midst of general cataclysm."[27]

But the very *douceur* and self-flattery of this situation should put the analysts of the perverse effect, as well as the rest of us, on guard: could they be embracing the perverse effect for the express purpose of feeling good about themselves? Are they not being unduly arrogant when they are portraying ordinary humans as groping in the dark, while in contrast they themselves are made to look so remarkably perspicacious? And, finally, are they not rendering their task too easy by focusing on just one privileged and simplistic outcome of a program or a policy—the opposite of the intended one? For it can be argued that the perverse effect, which appears to be a mere variant of the concept of unintended consequences, is in one important respect its denial and even betrayal. The concept of unintended consequences originally introduced uncertainty and open-endedness into social thought, but in an escape from their new freedom the purveyors of the perverse effect retreat to viewing the social universe as once again wholly predictable.

It is tempting to speculate further on the genealogy of the perverse effect. As already noted, its explicit formulation by Maistre, Müller, and others received a considerable boost from the sequence of events during the French Revolution, but its influence on our way of thinking may well have more ancient roots.

One underlying story is familiar from Greek mythology. Man undertakes an action and is successful at first, but success leads to arrogance and, in due course, to setback, defeat, disaster. This is the famous Hubris-Nemesis sequence. Punishment for man's arrogance and overweening ambition is meted out by the gods, because they are envious or because they are vigilant guardians of the existing order with its sacred mysteries.

In this ancient myth, the disastrous outcome of human aspirations for change is premised on divine intervention. Hobbes went along with this conception when he wrote that those who pretend "to do no more than reform the Common-wealth shall find they do thereby destroy it . . . This desire of change is like the breach of the first of God's Commandments."[28] In contrast to Hobbes, the Age of Enlightenment had an elevated idea of man's ability to change and improve society; moreover, it saw nothing but superstition in ancient myths and stories of divine intervention. So if the idea of hubris being followed by nemesis was to survive, it needed to be secularized and rationalized. That need was met to perfection by the late-eighteenth-century notion of human actions giving rise to unintended effects—particularly if perversity was the final outcome. With this new "sociological" insight resort to metaphysical argument was no longer necessary, even though the language of Divine Providence continued to be heavily used by figures such as Maistre.

The perverse effect has therefore numerous intellectual appeals and is backed up by deeply rooted myths. None of this is meant to deny that purposive social action does occasionally have perverse effects. But by intimating that the effect is likely to be invoked for reasons that have little to do with its intrinsic truth value, I intend to raise some doubts about its occurring with the frequency that is claimed. I shall now bolster these doubts in a more straightforward way by suggesting that the perverse effect is by no means the only conceivable variety of unintended consequences and side effects.

These two terms are in fact somewhat unfortunate, for they have contributed to narrowing our field of vision. In the passage of the *Wealth of Nations* where Adam Smith introduces the Invisible Hand, he speaks of an individual who, by acting in his own interest, "promote[s] an end *which was no part of his intention*" (emphasis added). In the context that end was of course a good one—an increase in society's "annual produce." But once the Smithian concept became famous and evolved into "unanticipated" or "unintended" consequences, it soon acquired a predominantly negative connotation, as "unintended" easily slides over to "undesired" and from there to "undesirable."*

---

*This shift in meaning took place in spite of Robert Merton's warning that "*unforeseen* consequences should not be identified with consequences which are necessarily undesirable." See his classic article, "The Unanticipated Consequences of Purposive Social Action," *American Sociological Review* 1 (December 1936): 895. Emphasis in original.

The story of the term "side effect" is less complicated. It simply has *kept* the derogatory connotation it had in its original realm, medical and particularly pharmaceutical science. The side effect of a drug is virtually always something injurious that must be set against the drug's direct effectiveness in curing a specific affliction. Thus both terms have or have acquired negative connotations that make them into close relatives, though by no means synonyms, of the perverse effect.

Actually, it is obvious that there are many unintended consequences or side effects of human actions that are *welcome* rather than the opposite, quite apart from the one signaled by Adam Smith. An example that is familiar to students of European economic and social history is the positive effect on literacy of universal military service. Similarly, the institution of compulsory public education made it possible for many women to take on employment—certainly an unanticipated and presumably a largely positive development. We simply have not paid much attention to such welcome unintended effects, as they do not pose problems that have to be urgently addressed and "solved."

In considering the full range of possibilities, we need to take account also of those actions, policies, or inventions that are comparatively devoid of unintended consequences, welcome or otherwise. These situations tend to be entirely neglected. For example, those who emphasize the perverse incentives contained in unemployment benefits or welfare payments never mention that large areas of social assistance are fairly impervious to the "supply response" that is at the bottom of whatever perverse effect may be at work: people are unlikely to gouge out their eyes in order to qualify for the corresponding social security or tax benefits. When industrial accident insurance was first introduced into the major industrial countries of Europe toward the end of the nineteenth century, there were many claims, on the part of employers and various "experts," that workers were mutilating themselves on purpose, but in due course these reports were found to be highly exaggerated.[29]

Next, there are cases where "purposive social action"— to use Robert Merton's phrase—has both favorable and unfavorable unintended effects, with the balance being in considerable doubt. But in these situations, the bias favoring the perception of negative side effects makes for a rush to judgment, with perversity being the sentence that is usually handed down.

The discussion around alleged perverse effects of welfare-state policies in the United States can serve as an example of this bias. Unemployment insurance makes it possible for a worker who has been laid off to wait before taking another job. In some cases this ability to wait may induce "laziness," in the sense that no intensive search for a new job is undertaken for some time, but unemployment insurance also permits a worker not to accept "work at any job, no matter how harsh the terms,"[30] and up to a point this is a welcome development. This side effect may even have been intended by the legislators and policy-makers, in which case they were less dim-sighted than they are generally made out to be. Similarly, the availability of benefits to nonworking mothers with young children under the welfare program known as AFDC (Aid to Families with Dependent Children) has been widely attacked because it not only assists already broken-up families, but tends in certain situations to encourage family breakup.

Here again the question may well be asked whether this particular side effect, granting that it exists, is always perverse. As was pointed out in a 1987 study, the availability of AFDC makes it possible for poor women to escape from marriages in which they are being brutalized or otherwise mistreated.[31] In this manner welfare assistance and the much-vilified "dependency" on it can counteract another kind of dependency and vulnerability: that resulting from oppressive family arrangements.

Finally, we turn to situations where secondary or side effects are sure to *detract* from the intended effect of some purposeful action. These situations are undoubtedly frequent and important, and with them we are getting closer to the perverse case. But the typical outcome here is one where some positive margin survives the onslaught of the negative side effect. A few examples will be useful. Speed limits and the introduction and compulsory use of seatbelts cause some drivers to relax their vigilance or to drive more aggressively. Such "offsetting behavior" could make for accidents, particularly among pedestrians and cyclists, that would not have otherwise occurred. But it seems unlikely that the total number of accidents would go up rather than down when regulation is introduced.* Irrigation projects designed to increase agricultural output in

---

*The perverse effect of regulation on the frequency of accidents was argued by Sam Peltzman, "The Effects of Automobile Safety Regulation," *Journal of Political Economy* 83 (August 1975): 677–726, but subsequent research has been critical of his thesis. While recognizing the reality of some "offsetting behavior," a 1986 Brookings study concluded: "There can be little doubt that passenger cars are safer today than they were twenty years ago. Most of this improvement occurred in the 1966–74 model years, precisely the period in which federal safety regulation was applied." See Robert W. Crandall et al., *Regulating the Automobile* (Washington, D.C.: Brookings Institution, 1986).

the tropics have many negative side effects, from greater exposure of the local population to schistosomiasis to eventual loss of irrigated acreage through waterlogging, not to speak of the conceivable increase in social tensions over access to water and distribution of newly irrigated lands. This potential for physical harm, material damage, and social conflict is likely to reduce the gross benefits that accrue from irrigation, but it does not generally cancel them out or produce a net loss. To some extent such damaging side effects can be guarded against by preventive policy-making. A final example, much discussed by economists, is currency devaluation. Designed to improve the balance of payments, devaluation will be more or less effective in this task depending on the extent to which the positive first-order effects of the devaluation are counteracted by its inflationary impact and other conceivable second-order effects. But as a rule such effects are once again unlikely to swamp the first-order ones.

Frequently there is in fact something intrinsically plausible about this type of outcome. This is so at least to the extent that policy-making is a repetitive, incremental activity: under such conditions yesterday's experiences are continually incorporated into today's decisions, so that tendencies toward perversity stand a good chance of being detected and corrected.

Almost two and a half centuries ago, Voltaire wrote his celebrated novel *Candide* to mock the proposition that ours is the "best of all possible worlds." Since then, we have been thoroughly indoctrinated in the power and ubiquity of the perverse effect in the social universe. Perhaps it is time for an *Anti-Candide* to insinuate that ours is not the most perverse of all possible worlds, either.

THREE

The Futility Thesis

The perverse effect has many appeals. It is perfectly suited for the ardent militant ready to do battle at high pitch against an ascendant or hitherto dominant movement of ideas and a praxis that have somehow become vulnerable. It also has a certain elementary sophistication and paradoxical quality that carry conviction for those who are in search of instant insights and utter certainties.

The second principal argument in the "reactionary" arsenal is very different. Instead of hot it is cool, and its sophistication is refined rather than elementary. The characteristic it shares with the perverse effect is that it too is disarmingly simple. As I defined it earlier, the perversity thesis asserts that "the attempt to push society in a certain direction will result in its moving all right, but in the opposite direction." The argument to be explored now says, quite dissimilarly, that the attempt at change is abortive, that in one way or another any alleged change is, was, or will be largely surface, facade, cosmetic, hence illusory, as the "deep" structures of society remain wholly untouched. I shall call it the futility thesis.

It is significant that this argument should have received its classic epigrammatic expression, *Plus ça change plus c'est la même chose,* in the aftermath of a revolution. The French journalist Alphonse Karr (1808–1890) coined it in January 1849, upon declaring that "after so much upheaval and change it is about time to take note of this elementary truth."[1] Instead of a "law of motion" we have here a "law of no-motion." Turning it into a strategy for avoiding change yields the well-known paradox of Giuseppe di Lampedusa in his novel *The Leopard* (1959): "If we want everything to stay as it is, everything has to change."[2] Both conservatives and, even more, revolutionaries have eagerly adopted this aphorism from Sicilian society as the leitmotif or epigraph for studies that affirm the failure and futility of reform, particularly in Latin America. But it is not only reform that stands convicted of failing to bring real change: as just noted, revolutionary upheaval can be similarly faulted. This is also illustrated by one of the best-known (and best) jokes to come out of Eastern Europe after the installation of Communist regimes there in the wake of World War II: "What is the difference between capitalism and socialism?" The answer: "In capitalism, man exploits man; in socialism, it's the other way round." Here was an effective way of asserting that nothing basic had changed in spite of the total transformation in property relations. Finally, Lewis Carroll's proverbial saying in *Alice in Wonderland,* "Here it takes all the running you can do, to keep in the same place," expresses yet another facet of the futility thesis, placing it in a dynamic setting.

All these spirited statements deride or deny efforts at, and possibilities of, change while underlining and perhaps celebrating the resilience of the status quo. There seems to be nothing in the repertoire of witticisms that mocks the opposite phenomenon, that is, the occasional demise of ancient social structures, institutions, or mind-sets and their surprising, at times outright comical, inability to resist the forces of change. This asymmetry tells us something about the association of conservatism with a certain worldly-wise wit as opposed to the alleged earnestness and humorlessness of the believers in progress. The conservative bias of the epigrams thus serves to offset the opposite bias of language with its derogatory connotation for "reaction" and "reactionary."

It is of course difficult to argue at one and the same time that a certain movement for social change will be sharply counterproductive, in line with the perversity thesis, and that it will have no effect at all, in line with the futility thesis. For this reason the two arguments are ordinarily made by different critics—though not always.

The claims of the futility thesis seem more moderate than those of the perverse effect, but they are in reality *more insulting* to the "change agents." As long as the social world moves at all in response to human action for change, even if in the wrong direction, hope remains that it can somehow be steered correctly. But the demonstration or discovery that such action is incapable of "making a dent" at all leaves the promoters of change humiliated, demoralized, in doubt about the meaning and true motive of their endeavors.*

Questioning the Extent of Change Wrought by the French Revolution: Tocqueville

The perversity and futility theses are likely to appear with different time lags in relation to the social changes or

*The perversity and futility arguments are compared at greater length later in this chapter.

45

movements which they gloss. The perverse effect argument can be made soon after those changes have been introduced. But with substantial or protracted social and political upheaval, it ordinarily takes some distance from the events before anyone will come forward with an interpretation implying that the contemporaries of those events were far off the mark when they interpreted them as fundamental change.

The French Revolution is a particularly striking illustration of this point. Contemporaries, both in France and elsewhere, experienced it as an absolutely cataclysmic event—witness Burke's statement, early in the *Reflections:* "All circumstances taken together, the French revolution is the most astonishing that has hitherto happened in the world."[3] It is not surprising, therefore, that any questioning of the Revolution's key role in shaping modern France in all of its aspects had to wait for the passing of the revolutionary generation. Such questioning came in 1856 when Tocqueville presented the thesis, in *L'Ancien Régime et la Révolution,* that the Revolution represented much less of a break with the Ancien Régime than had commonly been thought. Drawing on what was then deemed impressive archival research, he demonstrated that a number of highly touted "conquests" of the Revolution, from administrative centralization to widespread owner-operated small-scale farming, were in fact already in place before its outbreak. Even the famous "Rights of Man and Citizen," so he tried to show, had in part already been instituted by the Ancien Régime, long before they had been solemnly "declared" in August 1789.

This debunking thesis of the second part of the book, rather than the many insightful observations of the third

part, was widely taken upon publication as its principal
original contribution. For at the time, the raw questions
contemporaries or near-contemporaries of such events
cannot help asking—Could the Revolution have been
avoided? Was it a good or a bad thing?—were still very
much up for debate and indeed had acquired a new ac-
tuality, since France had recently succumbed again to a
Napoléon after yet another bloody revolution. In those
circumstances Tocqueville's findings about the many areas
of continuity between the Ancien Régime and postrevo-
lutionary France clearly carried political implications,
which were brought out soon after publication in two
important reviews of the book. One was by Charles de
Rémusat, a prominent liberal writer and politician, the
other by Jean Jacques Ampère, historian, close friend of
Tocqueville, and fellow member of the French Academy.
Rémusat puts the matter subtly:

> More interested in . . . day-to-day reality than in
> extraordinary events and in civil than in political lib-
> erty, [Tocqueville] undertakes without fanfare and
> almost without avowing it to himself, a certain reha-
> bilitation of the ancien régime.[4]

The point is made more explicitly by Ampère:

> Astonishment grips us as we come to see through the
> book of M. de Tocqueville to what an extent almost
> all the things that we look upon as the results or, as
> the saying goes, the "conquests" of the Revolution
> existed already in the Ancien Régime: administrative
> centralization, administrative tutelage, administrative
> habits, guarantees of the civil servant . . . extreme

47

division of land, all of this is prior to 1789 . . . Reading
those things one wonders what the Revolution has
changed and why it has happened.[5]

The second quote makes it particularly evident that, in
addition to his many other (greater) glories, Tocqueville
may be considered the originator of the futility thesis.
Futility took a special "progressive" shape here. Tocqueville did not undertake to deny that a number of basic
social changes had in fact been achieved in France by the
end of the eighteenth century; rather, allowing that those
changes had occurred, he argued that this had largely
happened prior to the Revolution. Considering the huge
travail of the Revolution, such a position was, to repeat,
more stinging and insulting to prorevolutionary opinion
than the direct assaults of a Burke, a Maistre, or a Bonald.
These authors at least gave credit to the Revolution for
having brought forth large-scale changes and accomplishments, even though evil and disastrous. With Tocqueville's
analysis the titanic struggles and immense convulsions of
the Revolution became strangely deflated, even puzzling
and a bit ridiculous in retrospect as one was made to
wonder what all the fuss was about.

Noting how the historiographical tradition has clung to
the image of the Revolution as total break (which was also
the image the Revolution had of itself), François Furet
puts the matter sharply: "Into this mirror game where
historian and Revolution take each other's word for it . . .
Tocqueville introduced doubt at the deepest level: what
if, in this discourse about the break, there were nothing
but the *illusion* of change?"[6]

Tocqueville proposed several ingenious solutions to the

riddle he had fashioned, as with his famous point in the third part of the book that revolutions are most likely to break out where change and reform are already vigorously under way. These are the most interesting sections of the book for the modern reader, but at the time they were perhaps too subtle to be accepted as a fully satisfactory explanation of the paradox.

The foregoing observations may help with another, smaller riddle: why has Tocqueville's considerable contribution to the historiography of the French Revolution been so largely neglected in France, in spite of the book's initial publishing success? It is only recently, in fact, that his work has been given extensive attention by a major French historian, specifically Furet. The reason for the odd neglect cannot be just that in France Tocqueville was long perceived as a conservative or reactionary by a milieu whose sympathies were predominantly with the Revolution and the Left. Taine's stance was far more hostile to the Revolution than Tocqueville's, yet his *Origines de la France contemporaine* was taken most seriously by Alphonse Aulard and other practitioners of the craft. Perhaps it was Tocqueville's espousal of the futility thesis that was responsible: later historians never quite forgave him for having raised doubts about the *pivotal* character of the French Revolution—the phenomenon to whose study they were, after all, devoting their lives.

Tocqueville's contribution to the futility thesis took a rather complex shape, which, I might add, largely exempts it from the critiques to be leveled against the thesis later in this chapter. A simpler formulation is also to be found in *L'Ancien Régime et la Révolution*. Close to the end of the book, Tocqueville speaks of the various attempts

49

since 1789 to restore free institutions in France (he presumably has in mind the revolutions of 1830 and 1848) and strikingly explains why these attempts have been unsuccessful: "Each time since [the Revolution] that we wanted to destroy absolute power we have succeeded only in placing the head of Liberty on the body of a slave."[7] This amounts to saying (to use a very different, contemporary metaphor) that the changes which were introduced were "merely cosmetic" and left the essence of things untouched. This straightforward futility thesis was not pursued at any length by Tocqueville. But it will be encountered copiously from now on.

Questioning the Extent of Change Likely to Follow from Universal Suffrage: Mosca and Pareto

Because the French Revolution was such a spectacular event, the dust had to settle before a deflating or debunking exercise such as Tocqueville's could be undertaken. The situation is quite different for the next appearance of the futility thesis, in reaction to the spread of the franchise and the consequent mass participation in politics during the second half of the nineteenth century. This spread occurred incrementally, unevenly, and rather unspectacularly among the various European countries and lasted for almost a century if the count starts with the British Reform Act of 1832. There was no obvious stopping point on the march to universal suffrage, which soon appeared to contemporary observers to be the inevitable outcome of the process. Under the circumstances the trend was subjected to criticism long before it had run its course, and a whole band of detractors came forward.

Some, such as the crowd analysts and Le Bon in particular, predicted disaster outright; others, again the "cooler," more acerbic kind, opted for the futility thesis: they exposed and derided the illusions that eternally naive progressives were entertaining about the profound and beneficent changes that were supposed to flow from universal suffrage and maintained that, to the contrary, universal suffrage would change very little, if anything.

As with Tocqueville's thesis about the French Revolution, this seems a difficult position to argue. How could it be that the introduction of universal suffrage into still profoundly hierarchical societies would *not* have considerable consequences? Only by arguing that the reformers were ignoring some "law" or "scientific fact" that would make basic societal arrangements impervious to the proposed political change. This was the famous maxim, put forward in different forms by Gaetano Mosca (1858–1941) and Vilfredo Pareto (1848–1923), that any society, regardless of its "surface" political organization, is always divided between the rulers and the ruled (Mosca) or between the elite and the nonelite (Pareto). The proposition was tailor-made to prove the futility of any move toward true "political citizenship" via the franchise.

Starting from different premises, Mosca and Pareto had come more or less independently to the same conclusion toward the latter part of the nineteenth century. In the case of Mosca, the immediate "sense data" by which he was surrounded as a young man in Sicily may have made it palpable to him that the mere extension of the right to vote would be rendered innocuous and meaningless by the island's powerfully entrenched landlords and other powerholders. Perhaps it was the seeming absurdity of

51

introducing what was an imported reform into a totally inhospitable milieu that led him to his basic point, first put forward at age twenty-six in *Teorica dei governi e governo parlamentare,* a book he was to rework, fatten up, and sometimes water down for the rest of his long life. The point was the simple, almost obvious, observation that all organized societies consist of a vast majority without any political power and a small minority of powerholders— the "political class," a term still used in Italy today with the meaning Mosca gave it. This insight—"a golden key to the arcana of human history," as Mosca's English-language editor wrote in an introduction to his best-known work[8]—was then put to a number of major doctrinal and polemical uses.

First of all, Mosca claimed with great relish that the major political philosophers, from Aristotle to Machiavelli and Montesquieu, had only focused on superficial characteristics of political regimes when they made those hoary distinctions between diverse forms of government, such as monarchies and republics or aristocracies and democracies. All of these forms were shown to be subject to the far more fundamental dichotomy of rulers and ruled. To build up at last a true science of politics, one needed to understand how the "political class" recruits itself, maintains itself in power, and legitimates itself through ideologies which Mosca called "political formulas," such as "Divine Will," "the People's Mandate," and similar transparent maneuvers.

Having debunked his illustrious predecessors, Mosca proceeded to take apart his contemporaries and their various proposals for the improvement of society. The power of his new conceptual tool is strikingly illustrated by his discussion of socialism. It starts with the seemingly unassuming sentence "Communist and collectivist societies would beyond any doubt be managed by officials." As Mosca notes sarcastically, the socialists have conveniently forgotten this "detail," which is decisive for a correct evaluation of the proposed social arrangements: in conjunction with the proscription of independent economic and professional activities, the rule of these powerful officials is bound to result in a state where a "single, crushing, all-embracing, all-engrossing tyranny will weigh upon all."[9]

Mosca's principal interest was in his own country and its political prospects. After the brief enthusiasm of the Risorgimento, the Italian intellectual and professional classes were greatly disappointed in the clientelistic politics that emerged in the newly united nation, particularly in the south. Armed with his new insight and given his special concern for that region, Mosca set out to prove once and for all that the—still quite imperfect—democratic institutions Italy had given itself were nothing but a sham. Here is his explanation:

> The legal assumption that the representative is chosen by the majority of voters forms the basis of our form of government. Many people blindly believe in its truth. Yet, the facts reveal something totally different. And these facts are available to anybody. Whoever took part in an election knows perfectly well [*benissimo*] that the *representative is not elected by the voters but, as a rule, has himself elected by them.* Or, if that sounds unpleasant, we shall say instead: his friends have him elected. In any case, a candidacy is always the work of a group of people united for a common purpose,

an organized minority which fatally and inevitably forces its will upon the disorganized majority.[10]

The futility thesis could not be stated more clearly. Suffrage cannot change anything about the existing structure of power in society. "He who has eyes to see"—one of Mosca's favorite expressions—must realize that "the legal or rational basis of any political system that admits the masses of the people to representation is *a lie*."[11]

Mosca's case against the emerging democratic institutions is remarkably different from that of his contemporary, Gustave Le Bon. Mosca sees those institutions as impotent, as exercises in futility and hypocrisy; his attitude toward them and their advocates is one of ridicule and contempt. Le Bon, to the contrary, views the rise of suffrage and of democratic institutions as ominous and dangerous because they will enhance the power of the crowd, with its unreason and its propensity to fall prey to demagogues. The franchise is derided by Mosca because of its incapacity to effect change, because of its foredoomed failure to live up to its promise and to give the people a greater voice; it is criticized by Le Bon because of all the disasters that are likely to befall the state should that promise be kept.

Yet the two theses are not wholly distinct. After arguing that the franchise would be unable to produce the positive changes its naive advocates were counting on or hoping for, Mosca managed to adduce several reasons why it might actually make things worse—in other words, he slipped from the futility to the perversity thesis. The malpractices that come with the manipulation of elections on the part of the "political class" would impair the quality of candidates for public office and would thereby discourage higher-minded citizens from taking an interest in public affairs.[12] Also, in a number of newspaper articles written in the decade prior to World War I, Mosca opposed the abolition of the literacy test as a condition of the right to vote for the tactical reason that the major groups of illiterates are to be found among the landless farm laborers of the south and that giving them the vote would only enhance the power of the large landowners.[13] It looks as though he had simply taken, once and for all, a violent dislike to elections, the vote, and the franchise and used any available argument to give vent to this emotion or to confirm himself in it.

Pareto's theory of elite domination as a constant of history is close to that of Mosca, both in its analysis and in the polemical uses to which it is put. It is already fully formulated in the *Cours d'économie politique* (1896–97); the much later *Traité de sociologie générale* (1915) adds mainly the theory of circulation of elites. Pareto's language, in the *Cours,* sounds at first curiously—perhaps consciously—like the *Communist Manifesto:* "The struggle undertaken by certain individuals to appropriate for themselves the wealth produced by others is the great fact that dominates the whole history of humanity."[14] But in the same paragraph Pareto distances himself from Marxism by using the term "spoliation" rather than "exploitation" or "surplus" and by making it clear that spoliation is due to the dominant class's obtaining control of the state, which is called a machine for spoliation. The crucial, Mosca-like result follows immediately: "It matters but little whether the ruling class is an oligarchy, a plutocracy, or a democracy."[15]

The point Pareto is really after here is that a democracy

55

can be just as "spoliative" of the mass of people as any other regime. Citing the example of New York City, probably on the basis of articles on the U.S. political system written by the Russian political scientist Moisei Ostrogorski and published (in French) in the late 1880s,[16] Pareto notes that the method by which the ruling or "spoliating" class is recruited has nothing to do with the fact or degree of spoliation itself. He intimates in fact that when elite recruitment proceeds by means of democratic elections rather than by heredity or by cooptation, the chances for spoliation of the mass may well be larger.[17]

According to Pareto, the advent of universal suffrage and of democratic elections could not therefore bring any real social or political change. It has perhaps not been adequately noted that this position dovetails remarkably with his work on the distribution of income, which made him instantly famous among economists when he first published it in 1896, both separately and in the *Cours*.[18] Soon after assuming his Lausanne chair in 1893, Pareto had assembled data on the frequency distribution of individual incomes in various countries at different epochs and went on to demonstrate that all of these distributions followed rather closely a simple mathematical expression relating the number of income receivers above a given income to that income. Moreover, the principal parameter (Pareto's alpha) in that expression turned out to have very similar numerical values for all the distributions that had been collected. These results suggested to both Pareto and his contemporaries that he had discovered a natural law— Pareto actually wrote, "We are here in the presence of a natural law"[19]—and his findings became known as Pareto's Law. The authoritative contemporary encyclopedia of economics, *Palgrave's Dictionary of Political Economy,*[20] carried an entry under this heading, written by the renowned Cambridge economist F. Y. Edgeworth, who had participated in the scientific discussions of Pareto's findings.

Pareto's success was soon emulated. In 1911 the sociologist Roberto Michels, who had been considerably influenced by both Mosca and Pareto, proclaimed an Iron Law of Oligarchy in his important book, *Political Parties.*[21] According to this law, political parties, trade unions, and other mass organizations are invariably ruled by largely self-serving and self-perpetuating oligarchies, which defy attempts at democratic control or participation.

Once Pareto had elevated his statistical findings about income distribution to the status of a natural law, important policy implications followed. It could now be claimed that, just as in the case of interference with the Law of Supply and Demand, it was futile (at best) to attempt to change so basic and invariant an aspect of the economy as the distribution of income, whether through expropriation, taxation, or social welfare legislation. The only way to improve the economic position of the poorer classes was to increase total wealth.[22]

The new law's principal polemical use was probably in controverting the socialists, whose electoral fortunes were then on the rise in many countries. As the editor of Pareto's collected works comments:

> Pareto's hatred of socialism infused him with extraordinary ardor: how fine a challenge to demonstrate, documents in hand, that the distribution of incomes is determined by fundamental forces . . . ! If the enterprise were crowned with success the solutions

57

advocated by socialism would definitely be classed as utopias. [23]

At the same time, Pareto's findings on income distribution raised considerable doubt about whether a reformist democratic politics based on universal suffrage would be able to achieve much more modest objectives, such as the narrowing of income differentials. In this manner Pareto's Law on income distribution yielded the same conclusions as his ideas about the state as a permanent "machine for spoliation": whether in the political or in the economic sphere, democratic aspirations are condemned to futility as they go against the immanent order of things. The polemical emphasis is on the naiveté of those who wish to change what is given as invariant by nature. But again, as in Mosca's analysis, the argument is enriched by a dash of the perverse effect. To go against the order of things is not just unavailing; for, as Pareto says in an article written for a general audience, "the efforts made by state socialism to change artificially this [income] distribution have as first effect a destruction of wealth. They result therefore in exactly the opposite of what one was after: they worsen the condition of the poor instead of improving it."[24]

Apparently the authors of the futility thesis are not quite comfortable with their own argument, however neatly it has been made: whenever possible, they look to the perverse effect for reinforcement, adornment, and closure. Even Lampedusa, master-strategist of social immobility, predicts toward the end of his novel that immobility will in due course be followed by deterioration. "Later it will be different, but worse. We were the Leopards, the Lions: we will be replaced by the little jackals, the hyenas."[25]

The contribution of Italian social science to the futility thesis is preeminent. Generally grouped together under the label "elite theorists," Mosca, Pareto, and Michels developed it systematically in many directions.* As already noted, Sicily's entrenched social and political backwardness made it tempting for Mosca to affirm that the introduction of universal suffrage would be unable to modify existing forms of domination. This disbelief in the possibility of change was at the core of Mosca's work, as was the corresponding belief in the unlimited ability of the existing power structure to absorb and coopt changes.

But Italy cannot claim a monopoly for this sort of reasoning. Oddly enough, the futility thesis can be encountered also in nineteenth-century England, then the outpost of economic modernity and gradual democratization in Europe:

> Legislate how you will, establish universal suffrage . . . as a law which can never be broken. You are still as far as ever from equality. Political power has changed its shape but not its nature . . . The strongest man in some form or other will always rule . . . In a pure democracy the ruling men will be the wirepullers and their friends . . . The leading men in a trade union are as much the superiors and rulers of the members of the body at large . . . as the master of a family or the head of a factory is the ruler and superior of his servants or workpeople.

*In his *Political Parties* (p. 355), Michels approvingly cites the Italian expression *Si cambia il maestro di cappella / Ma la musica è sempre quella* (There is a new choirmaster, but the music is just the same). This is an exact equivalent of *Plus ça change plus c'est la même chose*, with the rhyme thrown in.

Mosca and Michels are neatly rolled into one here, quite a few years before they put forward their own remarkably similar assertions. The quotation is from James Fitzjames Stephen's *Liberty, Equality, Fraternity,* first published in 1873, a wide-ranging critique of John Stuart Mill's essay *On Liberty* (1859).[26] It may have been inspired by the experience that the considerable extension of the franchise, achieved through the Reform Act of 1867, had not so far brought many changes in the way England was being governed, in spite of all the apprehension over the famous "leap in the dark" (see Chapter 4). But striking as the convergence here is with the ideas of the Italian theorists, the passage is not well integrated with the principal objection Stephen raised against universal suffrage on the much more conventional ground that "it tends to invert what I should have regarded as the true and natural relation between wisdom and folly. I think that wise and good men ought to rule those who are foolish and bad."[27] This sort of statement, rather common at the time among the opponents of the 1867 Reform Act and of universal suffrage in general, implies that the introduction of democracy would be actively injurious rather than that it would leave matters pretty much intact (the essence of the futility thesis).

Questioning the Extent to Which the Welfare State "Delivers the Goods" to the Poor

The conservative critique of the Welfare State is principally grounded in traditional economic reasoning about markets, the equilibrium properties of market outcomes, and the harmful consequences of interfering with these outcomes. The critique has pointed to the various unfortunate and counterproductive effects likely to follow from transfer payments to the unemployed, the disadvantaged, and the poor in general. However well-intentioned, such payments are alleged to encourage "sloth and depravity," to foster dependency, to destroy other more constructive support systems, and to mire the poor in their poverty. This is the perverse effect of interferences with the market.

Yet, for this effect to come into operation, the Welfare State must have at least one prior accomplishment to its *credit:* to generate the transfer payments and to have them actually *reach* the poor. Only upon this coming to pass can the unhappy consequences (of sloth, dependency, and so on) actually unfold.

At this point the outline of another possible critique emerges. What if the transfer payments never reach the intended beneficiaries and are diverted instead, not perhaps wholly but in large part, to other social groups with more clout?

The argument has much in common with the Mosca-Pareto denunciation of democratic elections as a meaningless sham (in contrast to Le Bon's argument about the extraordinary dangers of unleashing the masses). It has the "insulting" quality which was noted earlier as a characteristic feature of the futility thesis. When a welfare scheme can be shown to benefit the middle class instead of reaching the poor, its promoters are exposed not just as naively unaware of conceivable perverse side effects; rather, they will come under suspicion of being self-serving either by promoting the scheme from the start with the intent of feathering their own nest or, somewhat more charitably, by *learning* to divert a good part of the funds, once available, to their own pockets.

Clearly, to the extent that this sort of argument could be marshalled with some degree of plausibility, it would make a devastating case. The claims on behalf of the Welfare State would be shown up as fraudulent and it would be its critics who, rather than appearing to lack in compassion, would be able to pose as the real defenders of the poor against grasping, parasitic special interests.

However attractive it may be for the opponents of Welfare State legislation to invoke this argument, the extent to which it has actually been used in recent years is limited. There are two major reasons. First of all, this time the futility thesis is too obviously inconsistent with the perverse effect argument. It requires special gifts of sophistry to argue at one and the same time that welfare payments have those highly advertised perverse effects on the behavior pattern of the poor *and* that they do not reach these same poor. The second reason is specific to the debate in the United States. The principal debate on welfare reform has here been concerned with those programs—primarily AFDC—whose beneficiaries have to pass a means test; in the absence of vast mismanagement or corruption, the likelihood of such programs being diverted to the nonpoor is rather small. Consequently the main burden of the economic and political case against the Welfare State must be carried by other arguments.

The futility or "diversion" argument has nevertheless played an important subsidiary role in the debate. This was particularly evident during the days of Lyndon Johnson's Great Society, when the charge was often heard that many of the newer social welfare programs served primarily to provide jobs to a large group of administrators, social workers, and sundry professionals who were pictured as power-hungry bureaucrats wholly dedicated to expanding their bureaus and perquisites. The means-tested welfare programs, whose disbursements to the poor normally should escape the strictures of the diversion argument, actually are quite vulnerable to it. Their administration is more labor-intensive than is true of the categorical, insurance-type programs where eligibility is triggered by fairly clear-cut events or criteria, such as age, loss of job, accident, sickness, or death.

The futility thesis, in the shape of the just-noted diversion argument, has on occasion been put forward as a general critique of the Welfare State. An early example is a brief but influential article by George Stigler, Nobel Prize–winning economist from Chicago, in 1970. It was entitled, a bit mysteriously, "Director's Law of Public Income Redistribution."[28] "Director," it turns out, is the name of a fellow Chicago economist (Aaron Director, Milton Friedman's brother-in-law), whom Stigler credits with having enunciated a "Law"—probably in conversation, as no reference is given or can be found in Director's published writings. According to Stigler, Director held that "public expenditures are made for the primary benefit of the middle classes, and financed with taxes which are borne in considerable part by the poor and rich." Early in his article, however, Stigler disregards the role of the rich and argues primarily that public expenditures for such purposes as education, housing, and social security represent, if considered in conjunction with the taxes that finance them, state-mandated income transfers from the poor to the middle class. How can such a state of affairs come about in a democracy? Stigler's explanation is simple. The middle class first maneuvers the voting system so as to reduce turnout of the poor by means of literacy and registration requirements and the like; once in control of political power, it molds the fiscal system so as to suit its corporate interests. Some empirical evidence is cited: higher education, in California and elsewhere, is subsidized by the state out of general revenue, but the benefits of the university system accrue mostly to the children of the middle and upper classes; similarly, police protection serves primarily the propertied classes; and so on.

This sort of argument is of course familiar from the Marxist tradition which, at least in its more primitive or "vulgar" version, views the state as the "Executive Committee of the bourgeoisie" and denounces as hypocrisy any claim that it may conceivably serve the general or public interest. It comes as something of a surprise to encounter so "subversive" a reasoning among certain pillars of the "free-enterprise" system. But this is not the first time that shared hatreds make for strange bedfellowship. The hatred that is being shared in this case is directed against the attempt at reforming some unfortunate or unjust features of the capitalist system through public intervention and programs. On the Far Left, such programs are criticized because it is feared that any success they might have would reduce revolutionary zeal. On the Right, or among the more orthodox economists, they are subject to criticism and mockery because any intervention of the state, particularly any increase in public expenditures for purposes other than law, order, and perhaps defense, is considered as noxious or futile interference with a system that is supposed to be self-equilibrating.

Stigler's "Director's Law" was to be frequently invoked, with or without proper acknowledgment, in the subsequent years of stepped-up assault on the Welfare State. In 1979 Milton and Rose Friedman published *Free to Choose,* containing a chapter entitled "Cradle to Grave." Here they wrote, among numerous other anti–Welfare State arguments:

Many programs tend to benefit middle- and upper-income groups rather than the poor for whom they are supposedly intended. The poor tend to lack not only the skills valued in the market, but also the skills required to be successful in the political scramble for funds. Indeed, their disadvantage in the political market is likely to be greater than in the economic. Once well-meaning reformers who may have helped to get a welfare measure enacted have gone on to their next reform, the poor are left to fend for themselves and they will almost always be overpowered.[29]

The same argument was given book-length treatment a few years later by Gordon Tullock. The title of the book, *Welfare for the Well-to-Do,*[30] left nothing to the imagination. It does not seem to have had much of an impact, perhaps for that very reason, or perhaps because it marshalled even fewer data than Stigler's ten-page article. This is also true of the expanded treatment Tullock provided in his *Economics of Income Redistribution.*[31] The only empirical support for the argument was the assertion that in England the death rate of the poor went *up* rather than down after the introduction of the National Health Service[32]—once again a proponent of the futility argument felt the need

65

to add a dash of the perversity argument for greater rhetorical effect.

Whereas an isolated statistic such as the one just cited is of course incapable of proving anything, a serious study of one of the major social welfare programs in the United States did raise considerable concern about a substantial portion of Welfare State–sponsored transfer payments ending up with the middle- or even upper-income groups for which they had hardly been intended. In 1974 Martin Feldstein—later to become chief economic adviser to President Reagan—argued that this may be so in the case of unemployment compensation. At the outset of his article he said that he was writing to dispel a "damaging myth"— namely, "that those who collect unemployment compensation are poor or would otherwise be poor."[33] The "very surprising" statistics exhibited in the article showed that "the number of families receiving unemployment compensation and the value of benefits received is [sic] distributed among income levels in approximately the same proportion as the population as a whole. Half of the benefits go to the families in the top half of the income distribution."[34] Worse, Feldstein went on to show, if one compares the highest and lowest income receivers, the distribution of unemployment compensation is outright regressive! (More complete later estimates, reported in a subsequent note, corrected this particular "anomaly" and were in general much less "surprising.")[35]

Attempting to explain his strange and disturbing statistical findings, Feldstein suggested that the poor "are more likely to work in uncovered occupations, to have worked too little to qualify for benefits or to have quit their last job [instead of arranging to be discharged from it] . . . In contrast, middle and upper income persons are more likely to work in covered employment and to have earned enough to qualify for benefits for the maximum duration."[36] In general, middle and upper income receivers are of course better at extracting all the available benefits from the system.

Moreover, under a progressive income tax, the exemption of unemployment benefits from income taxation that was in force when the article was written was much more valuable for upper than for lower income receivers. This particular advantage accruing to upper income receivers was clearly an unintended windfall: the exemption dated from 1938, when income taxation was quite low and applied to only 4 percent of the population. The exemption stayed on the books for a long time out of sheer inertia. Then, in the late seventies it was gradually curtailed, in part under the impact of Feldstein's article; finally, in 1986, the new tax reform act included all unemployment benefits in taxable income and thereby put an end to an especially glaring inequity in the administration of this particular welfare program.

This episode certainly exhibits considerable "beneficial involvement of the non-poor in the operation of the welfare state," to use the apt expression of an English publication that analyzes and criticizes the phenomenon from the Left.[37] But the way the story unfolds in the case of income taxation of unemployment insurance departs significantly from the Director-Stigler script. A more charitable interpretation of what may be going on is also suggested by a welfare program that has been prominent in the developing countries.

In view of the massive recent influx of rural population

to Third World cities, particularly in Latin America, low-cost public or subsidized housing programs were undertaken in many countries, starting in the fifties. Initially the housing units built by these programs were almost everywhere far too expensive for the poorer families whose housing needs they were supposed to address. In consequence, this housing became available primarily to the middle or lower middle class. A number of factors contributed to this outcome: desire, on the part of politicians, to be seen *entregando una casa bonita* (handing over a nice-looking house); ignorance among the planners and architects of the projects about the kind of housing poor people could afford; unavailability of low-cost materials and building methods; and, particularly in the tropical zone, the alternative open to the poor to build their own homes, with their own labor and with a variety of very cheap, discarded, or "found" materials, on "free" land (obtained through squatting).

Subsequent programs to help the poor with their housing needs learned from this experience and were more successful in reaching the truly poor. For example, municipal authorities or housing agencies sponsored so-called sites-and-services programs: public provision and financing were limited to making available basic utilities on properly subdivided lots where the occupants were left to build their homes by their own effort. Finally, public assistance to housing came to be seen as most useful if it concentrated on providing public transportation and basic utilities for already built-up neighborhoods, however "substandard" and ready for the bulldozer they seemed to the eyes of middle-class observers.

A number of observations are in order. In the case of unemployment compensation, the beneficial involvement of the nonpoor had an important component—exemption from progressive income tax—that arose inadvertently as a result of developments occurring after the compensation scheme had been put in place. In the case of low-cost housing, it must be said first of all that even the housing that was unsuitable for the poor accomplished a genuine social purpose as it extended relief to the hard-pressed lower middle class in Latin American cities. Second, building low-cost housing and being criticized for its shortcomings became a valuable learning experience for public officials and housing agencies. It helped them to visualize the real dimensions of urban poverty. Eventually, traditional images of "solutions" to the "housing problem"— largely imported from the more advanced countries— were reshaped, and methods of public intervention were devised that had more of a chance to reach the elusive "poorest of the poor."

It appears on a variety of counts that the story of the beneficial involvement of the not-so-poor in programs meant for the poor is both more complex *and* less cynical than is implied in the version which attributes the diversion of funds wholly to the greater clout or "elbow power" of the better-off. In particular, critical analysis of results achieved and "anomalies" (Feldstein's phrase) encountered by officials, social scientists, and other observers can play a significant corrective role in a continuing process of policy-making.

Reflections on the Futility Thesis

Futility Compared with Perversity

During each of our three episodes the futility thesis has become incorporated in rather different shapes of reasoning. In this respect it is unlike the perversity claim, for whose monotonous, almost knee-jerk enunciation under the most diverse circumstances I have already apologized. Yet each time the futility argument amounted to a *denial or downplaying of change* in the face of seemingly enormous, epochal movements such as the French Revolution, the trend toward universal suffrage and democratic institutions during the latter part of the nineteenth century, and the subsequent emergence and expansion of the Welfare State. The appeal of the arguments rests largely on the remarkable feat of contradicting, often with obvious relish, the commonsense understanding of these events as replete with upheaval, change, or real reform.

A considerable similarity in reasoning appears particularly between two of our episodes—the critique of democracy at the hands of Mosca and Pareto, and the critique of Welfare State policies on the part of Stigler and his followers.* In both cases, attempts at political or economic change are shown to come to naught because they disregard some "law" whose existence has allegedly been ascertained by social science. The ambition to democratize power in society through the establishment of universal suffrage is laughable in the eyes of Pareto, who had investigated the distribution of income and wealth and had found that it follows everywhere an invariant, highly unequal pattern that came to be known as Pareto's Law. With income being distributed in this law-given manner, and with ancient hierarchies having been dismantled by the

---

*The remainder of this chapter concentrates on these two incarnations of the futility thesis. They share a concern for political and social reform in the present, whereas Tocqueville's contribution was primarily a new interpretation of past events.

bourgeois age, it was obvious to Pareto that modern society was in reality a *plutocracy*—a favorite term of his, along with "spoliation." Vaunted democracy was nothing but a mask hiding the reality of plutocracy. In turn, Roberto Michels' Iron Law of Oligarchy was closely modeled on the ideas of Mosca and Pareto; and Director's Law, as enunciated by Stigler, can similarly be viewed as descending directly from the constructions of Pareto and Michels.

Pareto and Michels had no doubt about the lawlike character of the regularities they had uncovered, and Pareto in particular took obvious pride in having his name attached to them. It was in this latter respect only that there was some change during the subsequent manifestation of the futility thesis. When Stigler chose in turn to proclaim a natural-law–like regularity that rules the socioeconomic realm and invariably crushes attempts at income redistribution, he preferred to give it the name of a senior and somewhat obscure colleague. The humility Stigler displayed in this manner is perhaps accounted for by his desire to enhance the authority of the "Law" by *not* claiming it as his own. Alternatively, he may have wished to put some distance between himself and the regularity he advertised: after all, in the seventy years since Pareto discovered his law, the reputation of social science for being able to come up with truly valid "laws" had suffered considerable damage. In any event, the futility thesis was again put forward in essentially the form that had served Pareto and Michels so well—that of a law ruling the social world, recently discovered by social science, and acting as an insurmountable barrier to social engineering.

At this point a much more substantial difference between the perversity thesis and the futility thesis comes into view. At first sight it might have seemed that the futility thesis, just as the perverse effect, is based on the notion of unanticipated consequences of human action. Except that when futility rather than perversity is invoked, the unintended side effects simply cancel out the original action, instead of going so far as to produce a result that is the opposite of the one that was intended. But the futility thesis is not at all constructed in this way, as though it were simply a milder version of the perversity thesis. In its scenario, human actions or intentions are frustrated, not because they unleash a series of side effects, but because they pretend to change the unchangeable, because they ignore the basic structures of society. The two theses are therefore based on almost opposite views of the social universe and of purposive human and social action. The perverse effect sees the social world as remarkably *volatile*, with every move leading immediately to a variety of unsuspected countermoves; the futility advocates, to the contrary, view the world as *highly structured* and as evolving according to immanent laws, which human actions are laughably impotent to modify. The comparative mildness of the claim of the futility thesis—human actions pursuing a given aim are nullified instead of achieving the exact opposite—thus is more than compensated by what I earlier called its insulting character, by the contemptuous rebuff it opposes to any suggestion that the social world might be open to progressive change.

It is not surprising, then, that the two theses have very different ideological affinities. In Maistre's classic formulation of the perverse effect, it is Divine Providence that foils the human actors. By bringing about an outcome that is the exact opposite of human intentions, she almost seems to take a *personal* interest and delight in "sweet revenge" and in demonstrating human impotence. When it comes to the futility thesis, human actions are mocked and frustrated without this sort of personal pique: they are shown to be irrelevant as they run afoul of some majestic law that rules impersonally. In this manner the perverse effect has an affinity to myth and religion and to the belief in direct supernatural intervention in human affairs, whereas the futility argument is more tied to the subsequent belief in the authority of Science and particularly to the nineteenth-century aspiration to construct a social science with laws as solid as those that were then believed to rule the physical universe. While the perverse effect has strong connections with Romanticism, the futility arguments of Mosca, Pareto, and Michels invoked Science and were ideally suited to do battle with the rising tide of Marxism and the scientific pretensions of that movement.

The difference between the perversity and futility claims is well illustrated by some fairly recent developments in economics. In the preceding chapter I noted that the perverse effect is familiar to economists because it arises from the most elementary tenets of their discipline: how demand and supply determine price in a self-regulating market. Interferences with the market, such as rent controls or minimum wage legislation, are well-known classroom examples of counterproductive human actions, that is, of the perverse effect. Most economists agree that, in the absence of compelling arguments to the contrary (minimum wage legislation being a case in point), economic policy should avoid quantity or price regulation of individual markets because of the likelihood of perverse effects. While sharing this consensus about microeconomics, Keynes and the Keynesians argued in favor of an interventionist *macroeconomic* policy on the ground that the economy as a whole may come to an unwelcome rest at a point where there is substantial unemployment, along with excess capacity of machinery and other factors of production.

This doctrine achieved intellectual and policy dominance in the early high-growth postwar decades, but came to be contested in the seventies, with the unsettling experience of rising inflation accompanied by economic stagnation and comparatively high unemployment. The counterdoctrines that became most successful within the economics profession go by the labels "monetarism" and particularly "new classical economics" or "rational expectations." From our point of view, the interesting fact about these attacks on the Keynesian system and policies is that they were formulated along *futility* lines rather than perversity lines. In other words, the new critics were not arguing that Keynesian monetary or fiscal policies would *deepen* a recession or *increase* unemployment; rather, it was shown how activist Keynesian policies would lead, especially if they were widely anticipated, to expectations and ensuing behavior on the part of the economic operators such as to *nullify* the official policies, render them inoperative, otiose—futile. Once again, this sort of argument is seemingly less extreme, but in the end much more galling.*

*To illustrate: in an interview where he discusses rational expectations theory, Franco Modigliani repeatedly uses terms such as "absurd," "offensive," "nonsense"; for someone who is ordinarily restrained and polite to a fault, this is strong language indeed. See Arjo Klamer,

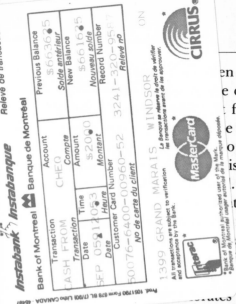

...en the perversity thesis and ...e degree of efficacy (or im-... first sight, once again the ...e stronger than that of fu-...o a desirable goal is actively ... is more damaging than if ... This is true enough, but ...ting the chances of success ...futility thesis is more dev-...sis. A world in which the ...ns accessible to human or ... out that devaluation of ...ates the balance of payments instead of improving it, why not experiment with exchange rate appreciation? Similarly, if it is found that the use of seat belts and speed limits really increases the accident rate, it is conceivable that things might be steered in the right direction by prohibiting seat belts and by compelling motor vehicle operators to drive at minimum rather than maximum speeds. In contrast, to the extent that the futility claim holds, there is no hope for *any* successful or effective steering or intervention, let alone for "fine-tuning." Economic or social policies are shown to have no grip whatsoever on reality, which is ruled, for better or for worse, by "laws" that, by their very nature, cannot be affected by human action. Moreover, such action is likely to be costly, and being an exercise in futility is surely demoralizing. There is only one conclusion to be

---

Conversations with Economists (Totowa, N.J.: Rowman & Allanheld, 1983), pp. 123–124.

drawn: the utmost restraint is in order insofar as any remedial policy-making is concerned and, wherever the futility argument applies, the authorities would do well to *bind themselves,* perhaps by constitutional rules, so as to resist the vain and damaging impulse to "do something."

Finally, the advocates of the perversity and futility claims have rather different ways of dealing with their antagonists. The analysts who come upon a perverse effect usually are so taken by their discovery and so desirous to claim it as an original insight and as an event *unanticipated and unwilled by anyone* that they are inclined to credit the policymakers whose actions have led to those untoward consequences with innocence for the disasters they have caused, hence with *good intentions* that are then disappointed. To convey this idea, they use the terms "well-meaning" and "well-intentioned" widely and condescendingly. Those who started the chain of events that led to the perverse result are portrayed as lacking, ridiculously and perhaps culpably, in elementary understanding of the complex interactions of social and economic forces. But at least their good faith is not impugned—on the contrary, it functions as the necessary counterpart of their incurable naiveté, which it is the mission of enlightened social scientists to expose.

With the futility thesis there is a considerable change. Once again, it is typically shown that policies pretending to empower the powerless (through democratic elections) or to make the poor better off (through Welfare State arrangements) do nothing of the kind and rather maintain and consolidate existing distributions of power and wealth. But to the extent that those responsible for the policies are right among the beneficiaries, the suspicion arises that they are by no means all that innocent or well-intentioned. Their good faith is being questioned, and it is suggested that the social justice and similar goals that serve as justifications for the policies pursued are nothing but smoke screens hiding the most selfish motives. Hence titles such as *Welfare for the Well-to-Do,* and aphorisms such as that of Lampedusa, cited at the beginning of this chapter. Far from being naive and full of illusions, "progressive" policymakers suddenly come to be perceived as cunning schemers and nasty hypocrites.

Yet the situation is not quite as neat as I have described it. The perversity claim, long associated with the view of interventionist policymakers as misguided but "well-intentioned," has lately been contaminated by the opposite judgment, which sees those policymakers as actuated by "rent seeking," that is, by the desire to spoliate (as Pareto would have put it) their fellow citizens through the creation of monopoly positions lending themselves to the extraction of monetary or other benefits.[38] Inversely, the promoters of the futility claim who "unmask" reformers as actually motivated by crafty self-seeking frequently continue to berate them for their enormous, if "well-intentioned," naiveté.

The Trouble with Futility

Whether or not the advocates of "progressive" policies and programs are naïve or selfishly crafty, the futility thesis thrives on "unmasking" or "exposure," on demonstrating the inconsistency between proclaimed purposes (establishment of democratic institutions or of redistributive welfare programs) and actual practice (continued oligarchic rule or mass poverty). The trouble with the argument is that futility is proclaimed too soon. The first evidence that a program does not work in the way announced or intended, that it is being stymied or deflected by existing structures and interests, is seized upon. There is a rush to judgment and no allowance is made for social learning or for incremental, corrective policy-making. Quite unlike the admirably reflexive social scientist, societies and their policymakers are taken to lack wholly the ability to engage in self-evaluation; they are also assumed to have an infinite capacity for tolerating what is usually known as hypocrisy, that is, inconsistency between proclaimed values and actual practice.

The main charge against the futility thesis must therefore be that it does not take itself *and its own effects on events* seriously enough. The story it tells about a wide and ever-widening gulf between proclaimed goals and actual social outcomes cannot possibly end there. As the story is absorbed by the listeners, it sets up a tension and activates a dynamic that is *either self-fulfilling or self-refuting*. The dynamic is self-fulfilling as the assertions about the meaninglessness of intended changes and reforms weaken resistance to their further emasculation and outright abandonment—in this sense, Mosca and Pareto can be said to have contributed to the rise of fascism in Italy, by pouring ridicule and discredit on the country's fledgling democratic institutions. Alternatively, the dynamic will be self-refuting as the very tension set up by the futility claim makes for new, more determined, and better informed efforts at achieving real change. The futility thesis thereby undergoes a notable transformation: it becomes remarkably activist, when its initial stance is that of a cool and mocking observer of human folly and self-deception; and whatever truth the thesis uncovers turns out to be ephemeral, when it was so sure that its pronouncements were based on some unchangeable "laws" of the social world.

Because of its contemptuous and debunking attitude toward "purported" change and progress, the futility thesis belongs squarely in the conservative camp. It is indeed one of the principal weapons in the reactionary arsenal. As may already have been noticed, however, it has a close affinity to arguments coming from the other end of the political spectrum. The conjunction of radical and reactionary arguments is a special characteristic of the futility thesis.

Whereas the perverse effect argument takes an extremely serious view of the political, social, and economic policies which it holds to be counterproductive, the futility thesis rather derides those attempts at change as inept, if not worse. The existing social order is shown to be expert at reproducing itself; in the process it defeats or coopts many attempts at introducing change or progress. This is the point where the argument shows a striking family resemblance to radical reasoning. The latter has often taken progressives or reformers to task for ignoring basic "structures" of the social system and for nourishing and propagating illusions about the possibility of introducing, without prior "fundamental" changes in those structures, this or that "partial" improvement, such as more democratic governance or universal primary education or certain social welfare programs. If some such features are in fact legislated, the next step is to argue that the preexisting pattern of domination has not really changed—it just has become more difficult to figure out its intricate functioning in spite of or perhaps *because of* the changes. At this point, heavy use is made of such metaphors as "mask," "veil," and "disguise," and the radical social analysts, like their conservative counterparts, obligingly provide the service of tearing off the mask, of lifting the veil, and of making us see through the disguise.

It never seems to occur to these critics that the tension between the announced aims of a social program and its actual effectiveness makes for a far more complex story than is conveyed by the contrast between mask and reality. The relationship that is implicit in this tired metaphor can on occasion change drastically, in line with the dialectic that some of the critics profess to admire: the so-called mask can manage to subvert the reality instead of hiding and preserving it. As I put it on another occasion, the more appropriate metaphor, originally suggested by Leszek Kolakowski, is in that case the Nessus tunic of antiquity, which burns him who puts it on.[39] In fact, through their denunciations of the gulf between announced policy objectives and reality, our conservative or radical critics are themselves busily weaving just such a garment. But it may be better on the whole that they are not aware of this role; otherwise their faultfinding might lose in action-arousing effectiveness.

Just once in a while one would like to see them a little less disabused and bitter, with perhaps a dash of that naiveté they are so bent on denouncing, with some openness to the unexpected, the possible . . .

The Jeopardy Thesis

The arguments of the perverse effect and of the futility thesis proceed along very different lines, but they have something in common: both are remarkably simple and bald—therein, of course, lies much of their appeal. In both cases it is shown how actions undertaken to achieve a certain purpose fail miserably to do so. Either no change at all occurs or the action yields an outcome that is the opposite of the one that was intended. It is actually surprising that I was able to account for a large and important portion of the reactionary arguments with these two extreme categories. For there is a third, more common-sensical and moderate way of arguing against a change which, because of the prevailing state of public opinion, one does not care to attack head-on (this, I have claimed, is a hallmark of "reactionary" rhetoric): it asserts that the proposed change, though perhaps desirable in itself, involves unacceptable costs or consequences of one sort or another.

There are several generic ways of arguing along such lines. Some of them were expertly parodied, early in this century, by F. M. Cornford, a well-known classical scholar at Cambridge University, in a brochure entitled *Microcos-*

mographia Academica.* Presenting his essay as a "Guide to
the Young Academic Politician," Cornford purported to
offer advice on how best to acquire friends and influence
by *opposing* any change in academic procedures while pretending to agree "in principle" with the reformers. In the
process Cornford distinguished between two main "Political Arguments": the Principle of the Wedge and the Principle of the Dangerous Precedent. Here are his whimsical
definitions:

> The *Principle of the Wedge* is that you should not act
> justly now for fear of raising expectations that you
> may act still more justly in the future—expectations
> which you are afraid you will not have the courage to
> satisfy . . . The *Principle of the Dangerous Precedent* is
> that you should not now do an admittedly right action
> for fear you should not have the courage to do right
> in some future case, which, *ex hypothesi,* is essentially

---

*First published in 1908, the brochure achieved considerable notoriety
in English university circles and has been frequently reprinted. While
lecturing in various academic settings on portions of the present book,
I was unfailingly referred to Cornford's essay by members of the
audience with an Oxbridge background. I am grateful to these people,
particularly to John Elliott, who lent me his copy of the second edition
(Cambridge: Bowes & Bowes, 1922). Cornford seems to be unique
among analysts of conservatism in sharing my interest in the *rhetoric* of
opposition to reform, rather than in the underlying philosophy or
Weltanschauung. I differ from him in that I convinced myself that the
subject deserved more than a purely jocular treatment.

An earlier and more diffuse attempt at cataloguing arguments
against change or reform appears in Jeremy Bentham's *Handbook of
Political Fallacies,* first published in a French translation in 1816, then
in English in 1824 and again in 1952, edited by H. A. Larrabee (Baltimore: Johns Hopkins Press). But Bentham was more interested in
refuting certain arguments he had collected over the years than in
examining their formal properties.

different, but superficially resembles the present one.
(pp. 30-31)*

Actually the two principles are closely related. Those
who argue along these lines do not contend that the proposed reform itself is wrong; rather, they claim that it will
lead to a sequence of events such that it would be dangerous, imprudent, or simply undesirable to move in the
proposed (intrinsically right or just) direction. What Cornford calls the Principle of the Wedge is perhaps better
known today as the "thin edge of the wedge" ("thin *end*
of the wedge" in British usage) and is implicit in several
related metaphors: a proposed move is just "a foot in the
door," or "the tip of the iceberg," or "the camel's nose
under the tent." The "slippery slope" is a related image,
widely used and abused. The wealth of metaphors testifies
to the popularity of arguing against an action on the
ground that, even though unobjectionable in itself, it will
have unhappy consequences.

Perceptive as Cornford's categories are, I shall here
pursue a different form of argument, based on the structure of the historical material I am dealing with. As we
know, T. H. Marshall used this material to tell an edifying
story of progressive expansion of citizenship rights over
the last two or three centuries, from the civil to the political
and eventually to the socioeconomic dimension. But this
tale of staged and cumulative progress virtually invites
attack and subversion on the ground that the passage from
one stage to the next is anything but smooth. In fact, it

---

*Cornford mentions briefly another common reason for opposing re-
form proposals: the reform, though intrinsically right or just, should
not be adopted because "the time is not ripe." This argument is charm-
ingly labeled the Principle of Unripe Time (p. 32).

has often been argued, progress in human societies is so problematic that any newly proposed "forward move" will cause serious injury to one or several *previous* accomplishments.

Here is a powerful argument against any *new* reform. When a proposal is acknowledged as desirable in itself, there is normally one major difficulty in attacking it persuasively by arguing that its costs or unhappy consequences are excessive in relation to its benefits. Such a statement involves a highly subjective comparison between heterogeneous benefits and costs. But if it can be shown that two reforms are in some sense mutually exclusive so that the older will be endangered by the newer, then an element of comparability enters into the argument and the evaluation can proceed in vaguely common "coins of progress": does it make sense to sacrifice the old progress for the new? Moreover, with this argument the reactionary takes on once again the progressive's clothes and argues as though both the new and the old progress were desirable, and then shows typically how a new reform, if carried out, would mortally *endanger* an older, highly prized one that, moreover, may have only recently been put into place. The older hard-won conquests or accomplishments cannot be taken for granted and would be placed in jeopardy by the new program. This argument will be called the *jeopardy thesis;* it should involve a more complex, historically grounded argument than the other two.

According to the Marshallian tripartite scheme, the civil, political, and socioeconomic dimensions of citizenship were put into place *sequentially* in the course of the past three centuries. To the extent that this construction captures the historic reality, one is immediately led to expect various kinds of jeopardy theses to make their appearance in the midst of those neatly staged forward thrusts. For example, an excellent opportunity to argue along the lines of the thesis arose when, in the course of the nineteenth century, it was proposed to expand suffrage and democratic governance in countries where civil rights and liberties were already firmly established. Opponents of suffrage might then be expected to conjure up the prospect that those rights and liberties would be lost as a result of the proposed advance of democracy. Next, when social security and related social welfare legislation were introduced, the opponents of these measures could deploy a double-barreled argument. The Welfare State, it will be contended by some, is likely to endanger earlier advances with regard to individual rights (Marshall's first dimension of citizenship). There will also be attempts to show how the Welfare State is a threat to democratic governance (Marshall's second dimension). Most often, the two arguments will be combined.

Marshall's scheme thus yields straightforwardly two distinct types of possible jeopardy arguments:

1. Democracy imperils Liberty.

2. The Welfare State imperils Liberty or Democracy or both.

Both of these claims have actually been put forward, and to that extent the historical validity and usefulness of the Marshallian scheme will be confirmed. But, as might be expected, certain countries will turn out to be privileged territories for deployment of the various theses. The reason is, of course, that the Marshallian sequential scheme was conceived in terms of British history and is therefore less applicable to countries where the progression from civil to political to socioeconomic rights was less steady, sequential, or "orderly." But the resulting variants of the jeopardy argument will themselves be instructive.

In other respects, similarly, our inquiry will not only confirm the continuing usefulness of Marshall's scheme, but will call its simplicities further into question. Marshall omitted to mention the powerful "reactionary" waves that rolled in, one after the other, to block and even reverse each of the successive extensions of the citizenship concept; he also ignored the possibility that these extensions may be mutually conflictive in various ways. The historical process he visualized was purely accretionary—one aspect or dimension of citizenship and progress after the other would be put into place, without raising any problem of cohabitation with the previous one(s). To the extent that the reactionary discourse around the jeopardy thesis turns up some real problems of this sort, our survey will serve as a corrective of Marshall's optimism and call attention to dilemmas and conflicts that are or may have been quite real.

Democracy as a Threat to Liberty

It is not exactly novel to question the compatibility of democratization, that is, of advances in political participation via universal suffrage, with the maintenance of individual liberties, the famous eighteenth-century "natural rights to life, liberty, and property." T. H. Marshall's distinction between the civil and the political aspects of citizenship has an affinity with several other dichotomies that, unlike Marshall's, have long been viewed in antagonistic terms. First of all, there is the distinction between liberty and equality; it closely resembles the Marshallian pair if, as is frequently the case, liberty is understood as the assurance to every citizen of his or her "natural rights," whereas equality is taken to be realized by the institution of universal suffrage. Even though this is a fairly narrow conception of equality, its potential for entering into conflict with Liberal liberty is considerable, and the potential is enlarged if equality is given a wider meaning. Ever since the French Revolution promised to realize both liberty and equality, and even more since the question of compatibility was forcefully raised by Tocqueville in his *Democracy in America,* the manifold tensions between the two aspirations have been thoroughly canvassed.

Second, the concept of liberty itself has proven to be so rich (and ambiguous) that it was shown to harbor distinct and antagonistic meanings. A famous exemplar is Isaiah Berlin's 1958 inaugural lecture at Oxford, "Two Concepts of Liberty," in which he opposed "negative" to "positive" liberty.[1] Negative liberty was there defined as the individual's "freedom from" certain interferences on the part of other individuals or authorities, with positive liberty being the "freedom to" exercise traditional republican virtue by means of participation in public affairs and in the political life of the community. There is, once again, a clear overlap between Berlin's concepts and those of Marshall: the civil dimension of citizenship has a great deal in common with negative liberty, as does the political dimension of citizenship with positive liberty. The interrelations and possible conflicts between positive and negative liberty have given rise to a lively discussion among political philosophers.[2]

Another famous distinction within the concept of liberty, that between the Liberty of the Ancients and the Liberty of the Moderns, had been drawn much earlier (in 1819) by Benjamin Constant.[3] According to Constant, the Liberty of the Ancients was the intensive participation of the citizens of the Greek polis in public affairs, while the Liberty of the Moderns was, on the contrary, the right of the citizens to an ample private space within which they could practice their religions and carry on their thoughts, activities, and commercial affairs. The similarity to Marshall's political and civil dimensions of citizenship is again obvious. But to a considerable extent, Constant saw his two kinds of liberties as mutually exclusive: only in this manner was he able to criticize Rousseau (and the Jacobin revolutionaries influenced by Rousseau's thought) for taking the Liberty of the Ancients as his paradigm and for pursuing therefore anachronistic and utopian objectives, with disastrous consequences.

This brief survey of dichotomies that are related to the Marshallian distinction between the civil and political components of citizenship conveys something of the richness and complexity of the topic which we are about to enter. It also holds out the promise of plentiful pickings for the jeopardy thesis.

Because of the vastness of the subject matter, I shall limit myself to a few important occasions on which the jeopardy argument has been put forward *in a specific historic context*. In other words, rather than enter the general discussion on the comparative merits and prospects of coexistence of democracy and liberty, I shall try to show how moves in the direction of democratic governance have been opposed, warned against, or bemoaned on the ground that they would endanger "liberty" in its various forms.

The exemplary case for the full deployment of the jeopardy thesis should be Great Britain in the nineteenth century. Here, at the close of the Napoleonic Wars, was a country with a long tradition of liberties successively won and consolidated over the centuries—Magna Carta, habeas corpus, Bill of Rights, right of petition, liberty of the press, and so on; at the same time, the country had an equally strong tradition of government of and by the gentry. Then, close to the one-third and two-thirds marks of the century, protracted and fierce battles were waged in Parliament, in public opinion, and occasionally in the streets, for the extension of the franchise, resulting in the two great Reform Acts of 1832 and 1867. With these battles taking place against the backdrop of long-established and highly valued liberties, the jeopardy thesis will in fact turn out to be paramount among the arguments marshalled by the opponents of reform both times around.

England: The Great Reform Bills of 1832 and 1867

The 1832 Reform Bill proposed to extend the right to vote to all male householders living in urban ("borough") premises taxed annually at ten pounds sterling or more. This and other provisions still excluded well over 90 percent of the adult male population, but admitted to the vote for the first time the industrial, commercial, and professional upper classes. The new monetary standard also introduced a universalistic criterion that superseded the traditional system based on family, clan, and ancient, often highly capricious, usage.

The remarkable feature about the eventual passage of the Reform Bill was that the aristocratic Whigs and their allies who favored it were just as hostile to *further* extension of suffrage to the "masses" as the die-hard Tories who opposed the bill. Both groups held that prospect in horror: it implied "democracy," a term then widely used as a bogey, in lieu of the progressive-sounding "universal suffrage." In his classic monograph on the 1832 Reform Bill, J. R. M. Butler noted in 1914:

> The word Democracy occupied in 1831 the position which the word Socialism holds today in a similar connection. It was understood to mean something vaguely terrible which might "come" and would "come" if the respectable classes did not stand together . . . something cataclysmic and all-pervading. If Democracy came, King and Lords would disappear, and old landmarks of all description would be swept away.[4]

Use of a generalized jeopardy argument of this sort was facilitated by the "Cult of the British Constitution" that had arisen in England in the eighteenth century.[5] With the revolutionary troubles in neighboring France and the powerful writings of Edmund Burke, this cult was considerably enhanced. One of its principal elements consisted in celebrating the delicate balance England had allegedly achieved in mixing elements of Royalty, Aristocracy, and Democracy. Opponents of the Reform Bill stressed that extension of suffrage would destroy that balance. More generally, it was argued that precisely because the "Constitution" had not been created by human intellect it must not be questioned or tampered with by humans or else the privileges of liberty enjoyed uniquely by the English people would likely wither and die. Many anti-Reform pamphlets put the matter in those self-congratulatory terms. One of them, for example, quotes from a speech by the eloquent and liberal George Canning (presumably pronounced on some other occasion, for he had died in 1827):

> Let us be sensible of the advantages which it is our happiness to enjoy. Let us guard with pious gratitude the flame of genuine liberty, that fire from heaven, of which our Constitution is the holy depository; and let us not, for the chance of rendering it more intense and more radiant, impair its purity, or hazard its extinction.[6]

With the Whigs and other supporters of the Reform Bill in the House of Commons sharing these concerns as well as the general aversion of the "educated class" to any substantial extension of the franchise, the only way they could justify the bill was by affirming and convincing themselves that the stipulated restrictions on the suffrage were going to be a *permanent* fixture of the constitutional order. In the last stages of the Commons debate, Lord John Russell duly made a "declaration which soon became famous stating that the ministers regarded the Bill as a 'final' measure."[7] A few years later, a contemporary observer (Francis Place) sarcastically observed:

> Lord Grey and his colleagues . . . in some inconceivable way persuaded themselves that the reform of the Commons' House could be, and as they framed it, would be "a final measure."[8]

The strange self-deception to which the supporters of the bill were subject perhaps owes something to the specific monetary criterion for the franchise onto which they had fastened. The key figure of ten pounds sterling for borough householders had the sort of "prominence or conspicuousness" among other possible numbers that made it conceivable for the line to be held there against future encroachments of "democracy."[9] Might not this figure acquire in time the authority vested in other elements of the hallowed British Constitution?

It was not to be, of course. Thirty-five years later, in 1867, after months of sharp debate and a number of bewildering realignments, the House of Commons passed the Second Reform Act, which became the decisive step in ushering in dreaded "democracy." It extended male suffrage to the middle class and even to parts of the working class as the vote was granted to all householders who had been residents of their town for a year or more. Substantial monetary restrictions continued for lodgers and people living in rural districts, and Disraeli still argued on occasion that the bill would be a "bulwark against democracy."[10] Yet he and his allies did not bother to assert this time that the remaining restrictions on universal suffrage were anything "final"; to the contrary, the Conservative Lord Derby, in his famous speech just before the decisive vote, frankly avowed that in voting for passage

Parliament and the country were taking "a leap in the dark."[11]

While the pro-Reform argument evolved in this manner, the rhetoric of the *opponents* of Reform remained firmly anchored to the jeopardy thesis. Indeed, use of the thesis became increasingly frequent as democratization proceeded during the last third of the century, at least until it became quite obvious that the extension of the vote to the popular sectors was *not* fatal, after all, to England's "ancient liberties." In the House the principal foe of the legislation was Robert Lowe, a Liberal politician who had served with distinction in the administration of Australia and was influential through his frequent contributions of leading articles to the *Times*. Breaking with the Whig leadership, he opposed passage of the Reform Act in several much-noted speeches, the most eloquent perhaps being the one he made on April 26, 1866. Its final flourish reads:

> I have now, Sir, traced as well as I can what I believe will be the natural results of a measure which . . . is calculated . . . to destroy one after another those institutions which have secured for England an amount of happiness and prosperity which no country has ever reached, or is ever likely to attain. Surely the heroic work of so many centuries, the matchless achievements of so many wise heads and strong hands, deserve a nobler consummation than to be sacrificed at the shrine of revolutionary passion, or the maudlin enthusiasm of humanity? But, if we do fall, we shall fall deservedly. Uncoerced by any external foe, not borne down upon by any internal calam-

ity, but in the full plethora of our wealth and the surfeit of our too exuberant prosperity, with our own rash and inconsiderate hands, we are about to pluck down on our own heads the venerable temple of our liberty and glory.[12]

This outburst brings to mind Madame Roland's famous cry, "Oh Liberty! How many crimes are committed in Thy name!" To be a fitting commentary on Lowe's speech and on many similar jeopardy arguments, it only needs to be modified slightly, to read, "Oh Liberty! How many reforms are obstructed in Thy name!"

Lowe's lyrical evocation of Liberty disastrously surrendered for the sake of the extension of voting rights was appropriate for the grand finale, but in the body of his speech he did supply some more detailed reasoning about the specific damage likely to result from the proposed legislation. The basic point is not unexpected: the extension of voting rights to the working class and the poor was widely thought to make in due course for a majority and a government that would expropriate the rich, directly or through spoliative taxation—it would thus violate a basic liberty, the right to own and accumulate property. Lowe puts it squarely:

> Because I am a Liberal . . . I regard as one of the greatest dangers . . . a proposal . . . to transfer power from the hands of property and intelligence, and to place it in the hands of men whose whole life is necessarily occupied in daily struggles for existence.[13]

Elsewhere Lowe cleverly invokes the considerable authority of Macaulay, who had been one of the artisans and most forceful advocates of the 1832 Reform Bill, but who was strenuously opposed to universal suffrage on the grounds that it could not but lead to the "plundering" of the rich. In a famous letter to an American correspondent, Macaulay had written, "I have long been convinced that institutions purely democratic must, sooner or later, destroy liberty, or civilisation, or both."[14] The argument was dual: the plundering of the rich consequent upon universal suffrage would in itself constitute an infringement on a basic liberty, that of owning property; moreover, the attempt to spoliate the rich was likely to lead to military intervention or to dictatorial government, with the consequent death of liberty. In confirmation of the latter sort of sequence, Macaulay made much of the way the institution of universal suffrage in France after the 1848 revolution was followed in short order by the regime of Louis Napoléon with its "despotism, a silent tribune, and enslaved press."[15]

Beyond the concern for property rights, fear for the stability of England's parliamentary institutions and for the maintenance of its civil liberties was probably a major objection to the voting reform and, in general, to "democracy." The fact that similar concerns of the opponents of the 1832 bill had proven unfounded during the subsequent decades did not deter conservative thinkers from arguing that, while everything had been going well enough so far, this time reform would bring disastrous consequences. The historian W. E. H. Lecky went one step further and in the 1890s constructed a golden age, demarcated by the dates of the two Reform Bills, in which England had dwelt all too briefly and which it had then foolishly relinquished: "It does not appear to me that the world has ever seen a better Constitution than England enjoyed between the Reform Bill of 1832 and the Reform Bill of 1867."[16]

Hostility to suffrage on the ground that it would endanger good government and "liberty" was shared, in the later decades of the nineteenth century, by other conservative thinkers such as James Fitzjames Stephen, Sir Henry Maine, and Herbert Spencer. Their views are repetitious and it would be tedious to go over them. Most of their arguments were articulated by Robert Lowe in the heat of the battle over the Second Reform Bill. Producing a number of variants of the jeopardy thesis, Lowe argued that "democracy" undermines intermediate institutions, that it threatens the independence of the judiciary, and that it increases the risk of the country's becoming involved in war.[17]

A particularly interesting facet of the jeopardy thesis is its deployment in the economic arena. One of Lowe's principal adversaries in the House of Commons was fellow Liberal John Bright, who twenty years earlier had known his greatest moment of triumph with the repeal of the Corn Laws and who, ever the reformer, was now in the forefront of the battle for extending the franchise. In the course of his speech of April 26, 1866, Lowe reminded Bright of the danger to which the earlier conquest of free trade would be exposed once the right to vote were extended to the so-called masses: "Look at free trade. If we have one jewel in the world, it is our free trade policy. It has been everything to us. With what eyes do Democracies look at it?"[18] A detailed description follows of the protectionist policies adopted in all countries with universal suffrage, from Canada to Victoria and New South Wales in

Australia, and mainly to "America," which "outprotects protection."

This particular form of the jeopardy thesis—democracy will jeopardize economic progress—was later given much emphasis by Sir Henry Maine in his militantly anti-democratic *Popular Government* (1886):

> Let [any competently instructed person] turn over in his mind the great epochs of scientific invention and social change during the last two centuries, and consider what would have occurred if universal suffrage had been established at any of them. Universal suffrage, which today excludes Free Trade from the United States, would certainly have prohibited the spinning jenny and the power loom; it would certainly have forbidden the threshing machine.[19]

Maine was so fond of this argument that he embellished it in another essay included in the same book:

> All that has made England famous, and all that has made England wealthy, has been the work of minorities, sometimes very small ones. It seems to me quite certain that, if for four centuries there had been a very widely extended franchise and a very large electoral body in this country, there would have been *no reformation of religion, no change of dynasty, no toleration of Dissent, not even an accurate Calendar. The threshing machine, the power-loom, the spinning-jenny, and possibly the steam-engine, would have been prohibited.* Even in our day, vaccination is in the utmost danger, and we may say generally that the gradual establishment of the

97

masses in power is of the blackest omen for all legislation founded on scientific opinion.[20]

Interestingly enough, much the same argument was to be used, some ten years later, by that other anti-democratic analyst already known to us, Gustave Le Bon:

> If democracies had possessed the power they have today at the time when the mechanical loom, the steam engine and the railroads were invented, the making of these inventions would have been impossible or could have taken place only at the price of repeated revolutions and massacres. It is fortunate for the progress of civilization that the power of the masses began to expand only when the great discoveries of science and industry had already been accomplished.[21]

Among the positive aspects of nineteenth-century experience, economic progress and a number of epochal technical innovations were no doubt the most important. By the second half of the century, the world and everyday existence were being visibly transformed by the railroad and other advances. Those who were looking for effective arguments against proposals for social or political change were therefore tempted to contend that such change would be pernicious to further technical progress. It was difficult to argue, as in the case of "liberty," that "democracy" would actually *destroy* technical advances that were already in place. So the next-best form the jeopardy argument took was: with universal suffrage there will be *no more* technical progress. Both Maine and Le Bon put forward this proposition quite independently during the last two decades of the century. The convergence is the more significant—in the sense that it testifies to the compulsion to argue along certain identical lines—as the argument itself was palpably absurd and was almost immediately proven to be so.

Enacting the 1867 Reform Bill was an extraordinary feat of "reformmongering," perhaps surpassing the more famous achievement of the voting reform of 1832.* In his biography of Gladstone, John Morley called the affair "one of the most curious in our parliamentary history."[22] A major paradox was the way passage of the bill was eventually achieved by a newly formed Conservative government, under the guidance of Lord Derby and Disraeli, rather than by the Gladstone Liberals who had originally introduced a milder reform bill. If in the end the Conservatives took the lead in electoral reform, many among them presumably disbelieved those prophecies about the dire consequences of enfranchising a substantial portion of the lower and middle classes that were made, along the lines of the jeopardy thesis, by Robert Lowe and his friends. Actually Lowe himself avowed here and there that it was the Liberal majority in the House of Commons rather than "Liberty" that was likely to come to grief if the act were to pass. Addressing himself to fellow Liberals, he warned that "a great many of these new electors are addicted to Conservative opinions. I do believe the franchise of the Government, if carried, will displace a number of most excellent gentlemen on this [Liberal] side and

*I introduced the term "reformmongering" in my *Journeys Toward Progress* (New York: Twentieth Century Fund, 1963) to designate processes of social change that are intermediate between the conventional dichotomous images of "peaceful reform" and "violent revolution."

replace them with an equal number of gentlemen from the other [Conservative] side of the House."[23] After the bill had passed, this was indeed the explanation sometimes offered for the part the Conservatives had played. As an opponent of the Bill put it:

> The phantom of a Conservative democracy was a reality to many men of undoubted independence and vigour of mind. A vague idea that the poorer men are, the more easily they are influenced by the rich . . . that the ruder class of minds would be more sensitive to traditional emotions . . . all these arguments . . . went to make up the clear conviction of the mass of the Conservative party.[24]

It was precisely on such grounds that Mosca was later to *oppose* the extension of universal suffrage in Italy: he argued, as we have seen, that the abolition of literacy tests would enfranchise primarily the rural masses of the South, whose vote would then be bought or otherwise dictated by semifeudal powerholders. So if it did anything, a wider suffrage would *strengthen* the power of the ruling groups.

In the England of the second half of the nineteenth century, conditions were of course very different from those in the economically and politically backward Mezzogiorno. But it was perhaps just because individual freedoms had long been solidly entrenched while the mass of the people were thought to be, as Walter Bagehot liked to put it, "deferential" as well as "dull," that the reality of the dangers conjured up by Lowe met with disbelief. As noted in the last chapter, even conservatives like James Fitzjames Stephen would on occasion criticize extension of suffrage along the lines of futility rather than perversity or jeopardy.

Moreover, the appeal to the dangers for liberty made by the opponents of reform could be neutralized by other hypothetical dangers evoked by supporters of the bill. To the dangers of action it is always possible to oppose the dangers of inaction. One form this typically "progressive" argument took was to affirm that in the absence of reform, the masses would resort to types of action that would be infinitely more dangerous to established society than the vote. This important point was made by Leslie Stephen, the liberal brother of James Fitzjames Stephen who was cited earlier as an exponent of the futility thesis. Leslie Stephen argued for the vote as a means to direct popular energies into comparatively innocuous channels and to delegitimize the more dangerous forms of popular protest such as strikes and riots.[25] According to this argument, it was the failure to enact the Reform Bill rather than its passage that would hold dangers for law, order, and liberty.

France and Germany: From Jeopardy to Incompatibility

The battle over the Second Reform Bill is the paradigmatic case for full deployment of the jeopardy thesis in reaction to the spread of the franchise. By the 1860s, according to a wide consensus of public opinion, substantial advances toward a well-ordered, economically progressive, and reasonably "free" society had been made in England, particularly in comparison to other European societies. Hence, it was only natural to worry that the proposed democratization of the vote would endanger those highly prized achievements.

In other countries the situation was then very different and progress from Marshall's "civil" to his "political" dimension of citizenship much less orderly. The case of France is of particular interest. That country was passing through several revolutions, reactions, and regime changes during much of the nineteenth century, so that individual liberties were far from being securely in place. As a result, the jeopardy thesis lacked plausibility—it is hard to argue that something is threatened when it is not there.

Moreover, universal manhood suffrage did not come to France after a long, drawn-out debate as in England. Rather, suffrage replaced virtually overnight the *censitaire* system of the July monarchy, during the first exalted days of the 1848 revolution. From then on, universal suffrage was never to be abolished formally. Upon seizing power in 1851, Louis Napoléon actually eliminated some important residence and similar restrictions that had been imposed in 1850 to keep the poorer strata from voting. Throughout his repressive regime he organized plebiscites on the basis of undiluted universal suffrage, thus accrediting the idea that universal suffrage, then often referred to as "democracy," not only does not go hand in hand with "liberty," but may well be antithetical to it.

Referring to the shutting down of a newspaper for which he wrote, Prévost-Paradol, a notable liberal of the time, put the matter squarely: "The progress of democracy has nothing to do with the progress of liberty and a society can become ever more democratic without even having a remote idea what a free state is like."[26] No wonder this sentence was prominently (if out of context) quoted by Robert Lowe, in the preface to the collection of his anti-Reform speeches in the House of Commons.

As a result of these historical circumstances, the jeopardy thesis in France tended to take a quite radical shape: it turned into the assertion that democracy and "liberty" are outright incompatible. One origin of this doctrine is probably Benjamin Constant's famous distinction, mentioned earlier, between the Liberty of the Ancients—the liberty (and obligation) to participate in public affairs— and the Liberty of the Moderns—the right to a broad sphere where one's private life and affairs can be carried on without interference or meddling on the part of the state. While Constant himself was fully aware of the need to combine these two liberties, the distinction he drew endorsed the notion of two wholly separate domains of liberty whose confusion (by Rousseau first, and then, in his footsteps, by the Jacobins) was alleged to have produced disastrous historical results. Almost a half-century later the separateness and incompatibility of the two concepts were reaffirmed, without any of Constant's subtle qualifications and reservations (and without any reference to his seminal essay), by the conservative historian Fustel de Coulanges in his influential work *La cité antique,* first published in 1864. In this scholarly and in many ways pathbreaking work of reinterpretation on the religion and institutions of the Greeks and Romans, Fustel makes it clear from the outset that he wrote the book with the express purpose of presenting Ancient society in general, and Ancient liberty in particular, as something totally alien to Modern understanding and sensibility:

We shall attempt to bring out the radical and essential
differences that distinguish these ancient peoples
from modern societies . . . as errors in this regard are
not without danger. The ideas which the moderns
formed about Greece and Rome have often misled
them. Having poorly observed the institutions of the
ancient city, they have attempted to revive them in
their own societies. They have deluded themselves
about the liberty of the Ancients, and *this is the reason
liberty among the moderns has been jeopardized* [*mise en
péril*]. The last eighty years of our country's history
have clearly shown that the progress of modern society has been held back to a considerable extent by
its habit of always keeping Greek and Roman antiquity before its eyes.[27]

Unlike Benjamin Constant, Fustel no longer allows that
the Ancients had evolved and practiced any important
variety of liberty whatsoever. In a later chapter he speaks
contemptuously of the political accomplishments of Athe-
nian democracy:

Having political rights, voting, appointing magis-
trates, having the privilege of being archon, that is
what was called liberty; but man was not the less
enslaved to the state for that.[28]

Equating "true liberty" with "individual liberty," Fustel
held that liberty was nonexistent among the Ancients—
they "had not even conceived the idea" of that concept.

The Ancients did not know the liberty of private life,
nor the liberty of education, nor religious liberty. The
common person counted for very little as compared

with that holy and almost divine authority which was called fatherland or state . . . Nothing guaranteed a man's life once the interest of the city was at stake . . . Antiquity formulated the disastrous maxim that the good of the state is the supreme law.[29]

Fustel's overt argument was, in short, that the famed democracy of Antiquity entailed a total absence of liberty, in the modern understanding of this term. To think otherwise was "the most singular of all human errors." The implied lesson from history was very much along the lines of the jeopardy thesis: imitate the Greek city-state, introduce democratic governance, and you will lose what liberty you have painfully gained. This position of course went far beyond anything Benjamin Constant had ever intended.

The idea that democracy was incompatible with the maintenance of individual liberties lost its credibility in England once it became evident, after passage of the Second Reform Act of 1867, that mass participation in popular elections did not cause any noticeable harm to the country's well-established system of civil liberties. But what about other countries? There the idea could perhaps be salvaged, particularly if the jeopardy argument were put in a more general form, such as: democracy is incompatible with *some* previous heritage, for example, with a cherished national characteristic.

Ideas of this sort can indeed be put together from various writings by both English and foreign observers. Their point of departure is a concern with what would be called today the personality foundation of democracy. Is there some human personality type that makes democratic gov-

ernance possible and some other that precludes it, so that
certain character traits would have to be *given up* for the
sake of democracy? Or, with different countries having
different "national characters," are there some whose citizens have less aptitude for democracy while being perhaps better endowed in, say, the artistic realm? Speculations of this sort became particularly attractive when, after
the Reformation and then even more with the French
Revolution, the political paths and experiences of leading
European countries such as England and France diverged
substantially and, it seemed, durably.[30] Efforts were made
to explain these differences by appealing to the contrasting characters of the English and the French. Burke engaged in this genre when he wrote brilliantly in 1791, in
an open letter to a French correspondent:

> Society cannot exist unless a controlling power upon
> will and appetite be placed somewhere, and the less
> of it there is within, the more there must be without.
> It is ordained in the eternal constitution of things,
> that men of intemperate minds cannot be free. Their
> passions forge their fetters.
>
> This sentence the prevalent part of your country-
> men execute on themselves.[31]

Here Burke puts forward a cultural-racial-climatic theory attributing the endemic lack of liberty in France to
the hot-blooded character of its citizens. In the *Reflections*
Burke had correspondingly stressed certain quaint traits
of the British: "our sullen resistance to innovation" and
"the cold sluggishness of our national character," as well

as the fact that "instead of casting away all our old prejudices, we cherish them because they are prejudices."[32]

To Burke these various traits (essentially the famous British "phlegm") are essential ingredients of the civilized political life of his country, as well as endearing foibles. It takes only a small shift in perception, however, to see them as a liability, or rather as a price to be paid for the maintenance of a free society. This step came close to being taken by Walter Bagehot who, some sixty years after Burke, compared the British and the French political systems and characters once again, this time on the occasion of another "convulsion" in the neighboring country, the February Revolution–June massacres–coup d'état sequence of 1848–1851. Bagehot's analysis of the difference between the French and the English is similar to that of Burke, with the difference that, through his paradoxical formulations, he makes the English appear rather less attractive than did Burke. Thus he speaks of "much stupidity" as "what I conceive to be about the most essential mental quality for a free people" and proclaims, almost paraphrasing Burke, that "nations, just as individuals, may be too clever to be practical and not dull enough to be free."[33]

A recent commentator has amusingly noted that some of the more outrageous passages of Bagehot, such as the ones just quoted, "should be asterisked, marked *pas devant les domestiques*."[34] Actually, it might have been more important to keep those passages somehow from unsympathetic foreign observers and, in particular, to mark them *pas devant les Allemands*. For a further sixty years and during another convulsion, that of World War I, a prominent

German sociologist, the usually astute Max Scheler, took up the same debate and argued that some of the personality correlates of democracy that had been described as endearing quirks by Burke and as paradoxical assets by Bagehot were actually serious and fundamental flaws. The comparison was now between the English and the Germans and the respective aptitudes for democracy of these two peoples.

In an essay first published in 1916, Scheler set out to counter the Allied claim according to which the war opposed the "democracies" to the "autocracies"; he asserted, to the contrary, that all "great nations" have evolved their own very different types of democratic forms.[35] In contrasting the English and German types, Scheler put forward a "tragic law of human nature" according to which the "spiritual liberty" of the individual necessarily stands in an *inverse* relation to political liberty: in Germany the "magnificent feel [*Sinn*] for spiritual liberty, spiritual breadth and for disconnectedness of the state from the most intimate personality sphere" goes hand in hand with "frequently all-too-willing subordination [of the individual] to state authority . . . and even with a certain tendency toward political servility," whereas in England the "emphasis on political liberty . . . , the traditional misgivings about interferences of state power and even the remarkable capacity . . . for promoting collective goals" have a negative counterpart in a "relative parochialism, intellectual narrowness, lack of feeling for the liberty of the highly original individual intellect, and in a for us Germans inconceivable . . . conventionality." According to Scheler, these various negative aspects were intimately and unavoidably connected with the positive ones; moreover, the peculiar bonding of positive and negative characteristics, or of virtues and vices, of the English and German systems would *never* come apart, at least not "as long as there still exists a unitary spiritual characteristic of that thing we call 'the German people' [*Volk*]."[36]

The idea of incompatibility—one kind of liberty can only be had at the cost of another—was formulated here in an extreme form. Unlike Robert Lowe, who argued along such lines to oppose the introduction of a new kind of freedom (the extension of the right to vote), Scheler imagined different nations choosing, as it were, among various available combinations of liberties and servitudes, each one according to its own *völkisch* genius.* This weird zero-sum construction illuminates, as I shall point out below, a basic (as well as a highly dubious) conceptual component of the jeopardy thesis—and operates, in the process, as a sort of reductio ad absurdum of the thesis in its more virulent form. The argument itself was obviously an outgrowth of Scheler's passionately nationalistic commitment during the war. In fact, immediately after the war Scheler excoriated, as a pernicious "German *disease*," the very combination of *Innerlichkeit* (intense inner life) with servility toward authority that three years earlier he had presented as a "law of human nature" and as an indelible characteristic of the German variety of democracy![37]

---

*This genre has a distinguished ancestry: in his poem "An die Deutschen" (To the Germans), Hölderlin characterized his compatriots, in a famous (and soon to be famously unfitting) phrase, as *tatenarm und gedankenvoll*—"short on action and flush with thought."

The Welfare State as a Threat to Liberty and Democracy

The argument that moves toward democracy imperil individual liberties was most fully articulated in England, during the second half of the nineteenth century. As already suggested, the reason lies in the uneven development of "liberty" and "equality" (in the sense of equal voting rights for men) among the larger European states: only in England were the individual liberties in place and could therefore—with some help from the turmoil in France—be presented as being vulnerable at a time when powerful political forces clamored for the extension of a then still highly restrictive franchise.

I now turn to a subsequent incarnation of the jeopardy thesis. The more contemporary and therefore more familiar claim is that it is the Welfare State that endangers individual liberties as well as democratic governance. Curiously, the first rumblings of this argument also originated in England, where the accusation was foreshadowed in Friedrich Hayek's famous *Road to Serfdom* (1944), written in London during World War II.[38] That the new jeopardy argument arose once again in England is actually not as fortuitous as it might seem. As in the 1860s, individual liberties (as well as by now democratic governance) were alive and well in the England of the 1930s; they could once again be plausibly portrayed as being threatened, both because they were extant and because they had recently been engulfed in another major "advanced" country, this time in Germany-Austria. And just as in the England of the 1860s strong demands had arisen for a substantial extension of the franchise, so the experience of the Great Depression in the 1930s had led in Britain to strong and, in part also because of Keynes's influence, newly persuasive demands for a more activist role of the state in the economy. At this point Hayek, with the authority of someone who, given his Austrian background, knew only too well the precarious nature of freedom, issued his eloquent warning that governmental interference with the "market" would be destructive of liberty.

There is one chapter in the book (chapter 9) that under the heading "Security and Freedom" deals specifically with matters of social policy. Today's neoconservatives would be shocked on rereading it, for Hayek goes surprisingly far in endorsing what was later to be called the Welfare State. He comes out in favor of "the certainty of a given minimum of sustenance for all," that is, for "some minimum of food, shelter, and clothing sufficient to preserve health and the capacity to work," as well as for state-assisted insurance against sickness, accident, and natural disaster. He criticizes, to be sure, a certain type of "planning for security that has such an insidious effect on liberty" and also warns that "policies which are now followed everywhere, which hand out the privilege of security now to this group and now to that, are . . . rapidly creating conditions in which the striving for security tends to become stronger than the love of freedom."[39] But at the time, Hayek's critique of social welfare policies was remarkably restrained in an otherwise highly militant work. Perhaps he could not help but share, or did not wish to offend, the overwhelming feeling of solidarity and community that was so characteristic of wartime England and that was reflected in the virtually unanimous endorsement by public opinion of the Beveridge Report, that Magna

111

Carta of the Welfare State, when it was published in late 1942, only a year or so before *The Road to Serfdom*.[40] As will be seen presently, Hayek moved to a much more critical position once wartime feelings had subsided and welfare-state provisions had actually been expanded in numerous countries during the first postwar decade.

With all its restraint, *The Road to Serfdom* nevertheless provided ample ground for *inferring* that the Welfare State jeopardizes liberty and democracy. The book was written primarily as a polemic against "planning" or against what Hayek perceived as a trend toward, or as pressures for, a more activist role for the state in various areas of economic policy, but the argument was couched in such general terms that it remained eminently serviceable when social welfare measures moved to the top of the reformers' agenda.

The basic structure of the argument was remarkably simple: any trend toward expansion of the *scope* of government is bound to threaten liberty. This assertion was based on the following reasoning: (1) people can usually agree on no more than a very few common tasks; (2) to be democratic, government must be consensual; (3) democratic government is therefore possible only when the state confines its activities to the few on which people can agree; (4) hence, when the state aspires to undertake important additional functions, it will find that it can do so only by coercion, and both liberty and democracy will be destroyed. "The price we have to pay for a democratic system is the restriction of state action to those fields where agreement can be obtained." This is the way Hayek put the fundamental point as early as 1938 in a paper which he mentions in his preface to *The Road to Serfdom* as con-

taining the "central argument" of his book.[41] In other
words, the propensity to "serfdom" of any country is a
direct, monotonically increasing function of the "scope"
of government. This simplistic argument has remained a
principal prop of the jeopardy thesis as applied to the
Welfare State.

Hayek himself went over to an explicit attack on the
Welfare State along such lines with his next major publication, *The Constitution of Liberty* (1960). It occupies all of
part 3 (chapters 17–24) of this work, entitled "Freedom
in the Welfare State." In the initial chapter of the part,
"The Decline of Socialism and the Rise of the Welfare
State," Hayek almost seems to regret in retrospect that he
was barking up the wrong tree in *The Road to Serfdom:* for
a variety of reasons that he expounds, his main targets in
that book, "planning" and socialism in its orthodox Marxist version, have lost a great deal of their attractiveness
for both workers and intellectuals in the postwar period.
But all is by no means well and there are still menaces to
be warded off: they are in fact the graver for being more
insidious, with the erstwhile planners and socialists continuing to aim at a "distribution of incomes [that] will be
made to conform to their conception of social justice . . .
in consequence, though socialism has been generally aban-
doned as a goal to be deliberately striven for, it is by no
means certain that we shall not still establish it, albeit
unintentionally."[42]

From this perspective, it is now the Welfare State that
is shown to be the principal new danger to liberty. While
some of the prudent formulations of *The Road to Serfdom*
are retained, as in a few initial pages of the chapter on
Social Security, Hayek deploys in effect a detailed, all-out

critique in his extensive subsequent treatment. Thus, Social Security is denounced in quite general terms because redistribution of income is now its "actual and admitted aim everywhere." And the main theme is again and again that of jeopardy: "Freedom is critically threatened when the government is given exclusive power to provide certain services—power which, in order to achieve its purpose, it must use for the discretionary coercion of individuals."[43]

The assertion that the Welfare State is a menace to liberty and democracy was not particularly credible when Hayek made it in 1960. During the first two postwar decades public opinion in the West had become basically convinced that the expanded social welfare legislation that had been introduced in most countries after the war made an important contribution not only to economic growth and to the smoothing out of the business cycle, but to social peace and strengthened democracy. The very 1950 lectures of T. H. Marshall on "Citizenship and Social Class" which have been mentioned so prominently here, consecrated the Welfare State as the crowning accomplishment of Western society, as it complements individual liberties and democratic participation with a set of social and economic entitlements. The consensus around this idea was well described by Richard Titmuss, who in 1958 wrote:

Since [1948] successive Governments, Conservative and Labor, have busied themselves with the more effective operation of the various services, with extensions here and adjustments there and both parties, in and out of office, have claimed the maintenance of "the Welfare State" as an article of faith.[44]

A very similar situation prevailed in most other industrially advanced countries. The overwhelming approval and popularity in which the Welfare State basked during a lengthy postwar honeymoon contrasts sharply with the widespread hostility that, as noted in Chapter 2, met the expansion of the right to vote in the nineteenth century. There were of course discordant voices, such as Hayek's, but in comparison to that earlier epoch, a remarkable consensus was achieved: the dominant view was that democratic governance, Keynesian macroeconomic management which assured economic stability and growth, and the Welfare State are not only compatible, but almost providentially reinforce one another.

All of this changed radically with the events—student revolts, Vietnam, oil shocks, stagflation—of the late sixties and early seventies. As a result, a refurbished group of jeopardy theses was soon to make a forceful appearance.

The immediate claim was not that the Welfare State endangered democracy or liberty, but that it was at odds with economic growth. Just as Robert Lowe and other British opponents of voting reform had warned in the second half of the nineteenth century that the extension of the franchise would undermine technical progress and free trade, those proudest achievements of the era just past, so it would now be argued that the Welfare State would jeopardize the conspicuous economic successes of the postwar period, that is, dynamic growth, low unemployment, and nicely "dampened" business cycles.

An alert was first sounded from the Left, ever attentive to emergent "contradictions" of capitalism. The by-then-dominant Keynesian thinking viewed economic growth and stability, on the one hand, and welfare-state expenditures, on the other, as mutually supportive—the expanded "transfer payments" were made possible by economic growth and were acting in turn as the famous "built-in stabilizers" that would sustain consumer demand in any recession.

This particular *Harmonielehre* (harmony doctrine) was implicitly challenged early in the seventies by James O'Connor in an article "The Fiscal Crisis of the State," subsequently expanded to a book under the same title.[45] Where others had seen harmony, O'Connor formulated the striking thesis that the modern capitalist state was involved in "two basic and often mutually contradictory functions": first, the state must make sure that continuing net investment, capital formation, or, in Marxian terms, accumulation by the capitalists, takes place—this was the "accumulation function" of the state; second, the state must worry about maintaining its own legitimacy by providing the population with appropriate standards of consumption, health, and education—this is the "legitimation function" of the state.[46]

Why should these two functions be contradictory, that is, undercut each other so as to produce "crisis"? In contrast to the neat syllogism of Hayek's proposition relating the increasing "scope" of state activity to the ruination of liberty, O'Connor never quite tells us, even though he makes much of what tendencies toward deficit budgeting, inflation, and tax revolt he could document at the time as the result of the expansion of what he called the warfare-welfare state. This term was of course designed to criticize the Welfare State from the left. In many ways, however, O'Connor's attack has much in common with critiques from the opposite side of the political spectrum, as can be seen from the following sentence which is perhaps the closest he comes to explaining his supposed contradiction: "The accumulation of social capital and social expenses [for health, education, and welfare] is a highly irrational process from the standpoint of administrative coherence, fiscal stability, and potentially profitable private capital accumulation."[47]

In the midst of the many discontents of the seventies, the news that a hitherto undiagnosed contradiction of capitalism had been discovered in America spread rapidly, no matter how shaky the underpinnings of the proposition. On the left, once again, Jürgen Habermas made extensive use of it in his influential book *Legitimationsprobleme im Spätkapitalismus* (1973), which was published in the United States under the more snappy and ominous title *Legitimation Crisis.*[48] But soon enough conservative opinion realized in turn its own close affinity with the O'Connor thesis. Only instead of seeing the increased Welfare State expenditures as undermining *capitalism,* it transformed the argument and claimed that these expenditures, with their inflationary and otherwise destabilizing consequences, were a serious threat to *democratic governance.*

In this shape the jeopardy thesis was freshly invoked against the Welfare State, and the problems of governance that had sprung up in various Western countries in the mid-1970s now gave it a plausibility it lacked when Hayek had appealed to it fifteen years earlier. The heightened political instability or malaise in various key Western countries actually had quite diverse origins—the Watergate scandal in the United States, the weakness of both Conservative and Labour governments in Great Britain, the sharp rise of terrorism in West Germany, and the post–

de Gaulle uncertainties in France. Yet a number of political analysts took to speaking of a general "governability crisis (or ungovernability) of the democracies" as though it were a uniform affliction. There also was much talk of "governmental overload," a term that insinuated the beginning of a diagnosis of the "crisis" by pointing an accusing finger at various unnamed undertakings of the state.

These concerns were so widespread that they were chosen as a field of study by the Trilateral Commission, a group of prominent citizens from Western Europe, Japan, and North America that had been formed in 1973 to consider common problems. A report to the Commission was drafted by three prominent social scientists and published in 1975 under the striking title *The Crisis of Democracy*.[49] The chapter on the United States, written by Samuel Huntington, became a widely read and influential statement. It put forward a new argument tending to make the recent expansion in welfare spending responsible for the so-called governability crisis of American democracy.

Huntington's reasoning is fairly straightforward, though not devoid of rhetorical flourish. A first section on the events of the 1960s appears initially to celebrate the "vitality" of American democracy that expressed itself in the "renewed commitment to the idea of equality" for minorities, women, and the poor. But soon the darker side of this seemingly fine élan, the cost of this "democratic surge," is laid bare in a lapidary sentence: "*The vitality of democracy in the United States in the 1960's produced a substantial increase in governmental activity and a substantial de-*

crease in governmental authority."[50] The decrease in authority is in turn at the bottom of "governability crisis."

What then was the nature of the increase in governmental activity, or "overload," that was so closely tied to this dire outcome? In the second section of his essay Huntington answers this question by pointing to the absolute and relative increase in various expenditures for health, education, and social welfare in the 1960s. He terms this expansion the "Welfare Shift," in contrast to the much more limited "Defense Shift" following upon the Korean War in the 1950s. Here he mentions prominently O'Connor and his neo-Marxist thesis, which also sees in the expansion of welfare spending a source of "crisis," and criticizes O'Connor only for having misinterpreted the crisis as one of capitalism—that is, as economic, rather than as essentially political, in nature.[51]

The rest of the essay is given over to a vivid description of the erosion of governmental authority during the late sixties and early seventies. Oddly, in his conclusions Huntington does not return to the Welfare Shift which he had identified earlier as the original culprit of the "crisis of democracy," and simply advocates greater moderation and less "creedal passion" on the part of the citizenry as remedies for democracy's ills. Nevertheless, any attentive reader of the essay as a whole comes away from it with the feeling that, in all logic, something needs to be done about that Welfare Shift if American democracy is to recover its strength and authority.

Huntington does not refer to Hayek,[52] even though he shares with him the basic view that liberty and democracy are threatened by the new intrusion of the state into the

119

vast area of social welfare. But the reasons adduced for the emergence of the threat are quite different. For Hayek, democratic consensus can no longer be achieved, as the state insists on taking up new activities so that coercion becomes necessary. This scheme had originally been fashioned by Hayek to demonstrate that what he called collectivist economic planning is either impossible or totalitarian or both. In reality the new social welfare activities taken on by various Western states in the postwar period, and then again in the sixties and seventies, resulted from precisely that national consensus which Hayek had decreed a priori as inconceivable. Huntington fully acknowledged the reality of this "democratic surge," but then claimed that dilution of authority and crisis of democracy were its unintended, unforeseen, and inevitable consequences.

The argument was actually an application to the United States of an earlier jeopardy-type thesis that had served Huntington well in his analysis of the politics of low-income societies. In various publications that established him as an innovative political scientist he had argued that economic development in these societies, rather than contributing to "political development," that is, to progress toward democracy and human rights, is bringing increasing demands and pressures to bear on existing and poorly institutionalized political structures, the result being "political decay" and military takeovers.[53]

The partial confirmation of his thesis by the political crises and upheavals experienced by numerous Latin American and African countries during the sixties and seventies may have emboldened Huntington to try an application to the "North," in particular the United States.

But here the evidence that there is a fearful price—in liberty and democracy—to be paid for thrusting new tasks on the state was at best ambiguous. The United States and other Western democracies that in the mid-seventies had been widely declared to be "ungovernable" and to be bent down, if not crushed, by "overload" continued along their respective roads without major accidents or breakdowns. And the topic of "governability crisis" exited from the common discourse as suddenly as it had entered it.

Not that the discussion around the Welfare State abated. On the contrary, more strenuous attacks were soon mounted, but they now directly impugned social welfare policies as counterproductive and wrongheaded, along the lines of the perversity and futility theses.

Reflections on the Jeopardy Thesis

Jeopardy and Its Associated Myths

"*Ceci tuera cela*" (This will kill that) is the title of a famous chapter in Victor Hugo's novel *Notre-Dame de Paris*. Here *ceci* stood for printing and the book, which, with the invention of movable type, would take the place, Hugo explained, of *cela*, that is, of cathedrals and other monumental architecture, as the principal expression of Western culture. Much more recently a similar downfall was announced for the book itself: According to Marshall McLuhan, "linear" printing and bookmaking were in turn destined for obsolescence, as "electric circuitry" in general, and television in particular, would take over.

Many similar prophecies of such joint rise-and-falls could be collected, but I shall proceed directly to making two general observations:

1. The prophecies turn out to be absolutely correct—except for the occasions when they are not.

2. As the frequency with which such statements are made is considerably in excess of what occurs "in nature," there must be some inherent intellectual attraction in advancing them.

In part this attraction is no doubt due to the Warholian promise of fifteen-minute celebrity that these predictions hold out to their authors. For example, when a new material (say nylon) begins to eat into the market of an older one (silk), it is not only easier but more arresting to announce that the process will result in the total demise of the latter than to explore the ways in which the two might eventually coexist and come to occupy well-defined market niches.

More generally, the frequent recourse to the *ceci-tuera-cela* type of statement may be interpreted as being rooted in a stubborn "zero-sum mentality." The zero-sum game, where the gains of the winner are mathematically equal to the losses of the loser, is of course wholly predominant in the world of games and has a powerful grip on our strategic imagination. Some years ago the anthropologist George Foster proposed a culturally more meaningful term, the Image of Limited Good, for this mentality. His studies of Indian peasant communities in Mexico suggested to him the existence of a widespread belief that any fortuitous gain in one direction, for an individual or for a group, is bound to be balanced and therefore in fact erased by an equivalent loss in another.[54]

Upon looking more closely, one frequently finds that the *ceci-tuera-cela* statements point to a *negative* rather than to a zero-sum outcome: we lose and we gain, but what we lose is more precious than what we gain. It is a case of one step forward, two steps backward: what first looks like progress is not just illusory, but outright impoverishing. These situations are once again similar to the Hubris-Nemesis sequence, where man is punished by the gods for gaining access to forbidden knowledge or for becoming too powerful, rich, and successful; in the end he is left worse off than he was before (if not dead).

The jeopardy thesis draws considerable strength from its connections with these various myths and stereotypes. The argument that a new advance will imperil an older one is somehow immediately plausible, as is the idea that an ancient liberty is bound to be more valuable or fundamental than a new ("newfangled") one. Jointly these two arguments make a powerful case against any change in the status quo. Perhaps it is because of their reliance on these easy and automatic connections of the jeopardy thesis with strongly rooted mental images that its protagonists have been satisfied with fairly flimsy arguments. Upon setting out to examine the principal intellectual episodes in which the jeopardy thesis was invoked, I confidently expected to meet with the more sophisticated among the various "reactionary" arguments that I would deal with in my survey. This expectation has been disappointed. Instead of the rich historical argumentation to which I was looking forward, the purveyors of the jeopardy claim, from Robert Lowe to Samuel Huntington, have often been satisfied with simple affirmations of the *ceci-tuera-cela* type. In the case of Huntington, for example, the primary link that is established between the Welfare Shift and the increasing "ungovernability" of the United States is the fact that they were properly phased, with the shift preceding the outbreak of ungovernability of the American democracy in the mid-seventies—an outbreak which then turned out to be rather short-lived. It is as though you are able to dispense with the demonstration of any more persuasive causal nexus when you can point to such a well-timed rise-and-fall sequence: there will be a collective jump to the conclusion that the two are intimately connected.

Jeopardy versus Mutual Support

The jeopardy thesis is only one way of establishing connections between two successive attempts at social change or reform. It is easy to visualize the opposite line of argument: that an already established reform or institution A would be *strengthened,* rather than weakened (as in the jeopardy claim), by projected reform or institution B; that B's enactment is required to give robustness and meaning to A; that B is needed as a complement to A. This *complementarity, harmony, synergy,* or *mutual support* argument is likely to be marshalled quite some time ahead of the jeopardy claim, for it will be put forward by the early "progressive" advocates of B long before B has become an imminent or actual reality that will then mobilize reactionaries and their arguments. This interval between the points of time at which the two opposite arguments emerge makes it conceivable that they never come to grips with each other.

The debate on social welfare policies is perhaps a case in point. When these policies were first advocated and adopted, a major argument in their favor was that they were indispensably required both to save capitalism from the consequences of its own excesses (unemployment, mass migration, disintegration of communities and of extended family systems) and to make sure that the newly instituted or expanded franchise would not be abused by the existence of large numbers of uneducated, unhealthy, and impoverished voters. These seemingly reasonable and even powerful earlier arguments in favor of social welfare measures were largely ignored by those who later on stressed the various ways in which the welfare state enters into conflict with capitalism, freedom, or the stability of democracy.

Yet it is hard to believe that the critics of the Welfare State who asserted the jeopardy claim and made in the process a *historical* argument were totally oblivious of the earlier harmony or mutual support claims. If they were right they would demonstrate, after all, that the earlier analysts were radically misguided: social welfare policies, rather than shoring up capitalism and buttressing democracy, were in effect undermining these formations. To generalize a bit: *A course of action taken expressly to forestall a feared event turns out to help bring it about.* There surely would be a special delight for conservative thinkers in exposing that sort of sequence. It manages to introduce perversity on top of jeopardy as action is shown to result in the opposite of what was intended. In fact, the sequence portrays "purposive" human action and planning at their most pitifully impotent—much like the story of Oedipus, where the King-Father's very activism, his attempt to avert the announced fate (by ordering the child Oedipus to be killed), is an important link in the sequence of events that cause the divine prophecy to be fulfilled. Well aware of and quite delighted by that sort of sequence, Joseph de

125

Maistre characterized it as a special "affectation" of Providence in his remarkable formulation of the perverse effect, cited in Chapter 2.

Abetted by still another myth, some partisans of the jeopardy thesis may thus be confirmed in their beliefs as they contemplate the mutual support argument and the astounding, yet to them comforting, extent to which humans can fall into error. But others may come to perceive that jointly the two opposite theses define a rich field of *intermediate possibilities* which contains most of the historically relevant situations. Once jeopardy and mutual support are seen as two limiting and equally unrealistic cases, it is indeed possible to conceive of a large variety of composite ways in which a new reform may interact with an older one that is already in place.[55]

One obvious possibility is that the partisans of mutual support and those of jeopardy are both right, but in turn: a new reform strengthens an old one for a while, but enters into conflict with it subsequently as the new reform is carried beyond a certain point. Or take the opposite sequence: the fight for a new reform creates a high degree of tension and instability and thereby endangers institutions that embody some antecedent achievement of "progress"; but eventually both the new reform and the older institutions settle down and in the process draw strength from each other. Such schemes, with jeopardy and harmony holding sway in neat alternation, are still quite primitive. More complex situations are not only conceivable but can claim to be more realistic. For example, any new reform program or "progressive" move is likely to have several aspects, activities, and effects, some of which may be helpful in strengthening an established reform or institution while others are working at cross-purposes with it and yet others would involve neither help nor harm. Moreover, whether and to what extent the new reform has these positive, negative, or neutral effects on the older one may well depend more on specific surrounding circumstances than on the intrinsic characteristics of the reforms.

In view of such complications of the "real world," it is unsurprising that discussions of the interaction between past and planned future progress should have been largely confined to the two limiting cases. To find feasible combinations of the new and the old, without laboring under the illusions of mutual support, while being alert to the dangers of jeopardy is essentially a matter of practical historical invention.

Jeopardy versus Getting Stuck

In spite of its close connection to familiar thought patterns—rise and decline, zero-sum, *ceci tuera cela,* and so on—the domain of the jeopardy thesis is more restricted than those of the perversity and futility arguments. For jeopardy requires as backdrop a specific historical setting and consciousness: when a "progressive" undertaking is being advocated or enacted in a community or nation, there must exist the living memory of a highly prized *earlier* reform, institution, or achievement that might arguably be endangered by the new move. This should not be a severely limiting stipulation. But some societies are simply more conscious than others of their social and political history's having passed through a well-ordered series of unerringly progressive stages. For this conceit they must, as it were, pay a price: they become the principal stage for the deployment of the jeopardy thesis.

The matter is related to a once much discussed topic in "political development." In Western Europe, so it was pointed out by various authors, the distinct "tasks" or "requisites" of nation building—achieving territorial identity, securing authority over that territory, enlisting and managing mass participation—were undertaken one after the other, over a period of centuries, while the "new nations" of the Third World are faced with all of them at once.[56] Similarly, the Marshallian story—the progression from civil rights to mass participation in politics through universal suffrage to socioeconomic entitlements—proceeded in a far more leisurely and "orderly" manner in Great Britain than in the other major European countries, not to speak of the rest of the world. This is the reason, of course, why the jeopardy thesis has been invoked primarily in England as well as in the United States—with the exception of slavery, the consolidation of individual liberties and of democratic institutions and the development of modern social welfare policies followed here also a well-delineated sequential path.

In the debate on so-called political development, the distinction between the few countries which were able to solve their problems one by one over a long period and the (presumably less fortunate) others for which that period has been highly compressed, served an obvious purpose: to demonstrate that latecomers face a daunting task, to convey an appreciation of the special difficulties of nation building in the twentieth century. Let us accept this argument for the moment. The latecoming countries are then seen to have at least one *advantage* on their side: when it comes to endowing them with, say, Welfare State institutions, it will not be possible to combat this advance in the name of preserving a tradition of democracy or of individual liberties, since that tradition hardly exists. In other words, the jeopardy thesis cannot be invoked in such cases.

The "rhetorical" advantage thus making life easier for the Welfare State advocates in the latecomers may seem a small consolation in comparison to the "real" disadvantage—the need to solve several problems of state building at once—under which latecoming societies are said to labor. But that disadvantage looks rather less formidable once the underlying argument is called into question.

To begin with, it is simply not true that the advanced countries always enjoy the luxury of sequential problem-solving, whereas latecomers are uniformly forced into a virtually simultaneous operation. Take the stages of industrialization: it has not been adequately noted, probably because of the lack of communication between economists and political scientists, that it is the inverse relationship which holds here. With capital and intermediate goods being available from abroad, it is the latecomers that, for a change, have been able to move leisurely, in accordance with the backward linkage dynamic, from the last stages of production to the earlier ones and on to the production of capital goods (if they ever get that far), while the pioneering industrial countries often had to produce concurrently all needed inputs including their own capital goods, if only by artisan methods. In this case, however, the compulsion for the pioneering industrial countries to occupy all stages of production at once has been considered an *advantage* (from the point of view of the dynamic of industrialization), whereas the sequential nature of the industrialization process among the later industrializers has been looked at correspondingly as a drawback, *because of the risk of getting stuck* at the finished consumer goods stage. These risks are real: as I have explained elsewhere, "the industrialist who has worked hitherto with imported materials will often be hostile to the establishment of domestic industries producing these materials" and, more generally, "whereas the first steps [of industrialization] are easy to take by themselves, they can make it difficult to take the next ones."[57]

Comparing the dynamics of industrialization and of political development seems to yield at first only one rather disconcerting generalization: whether the tasks facing the advanced countries can be tackled sequentially or must be solved all at once, these countries always have the better part of the deal. But that should hardly come as a surprise—it is one of the many interlocking reasons why these countries *are* advanced.

The argument nevertheless has its uses. First of all, it brings out a formal point: stressing the risk of getting stuck in the first or early stage of some process, of never reaching the subsequent ones, is the mirror image of the jeopardy thesis, that is, the insistence on the risk of damaging an earlier accomplishment by some new action. In both cases the exponents of these opposite worries think in terms of two successive stages that are alleged to be conflictive or incompatible. But there is a difference: those who fret about the risk of getting stuck view the second stage as a highly desirable, even essential consummation, whereas those who invoke the danger of jeopardy are in truth much fonder of the accomplishments of the earlier stage.

The comparison of the two dynamics permits a more substantial conclusion. Leisurely, sequential problem-solving is not always a pure blessing, as has been argued in the literature on political development.* Sequential problem-solving brings with it the risk of getting stuck, and this risk may apply not only to the sequence from the production of consumer goods to that of machinery and intermediate goods, but, in a different form, to the complex Marshallian progression from individual liberties to universal suffrage and on to the Welfare State. One does not need to believe in the jeopardy thesis (in the form, for example, of an absolute incompatibility between Welfare State programs and the safeguarding of individual liberties) to acknowledge that a society which has pioneered in securing these liberties is likely to experience special difficulties in subsequently establishing comprehensive social welfare policies. The very values that serve such a society well in one phase—the belief in the supreme value of individuality, the insistence on individual achievement and individual responsibility—may be something of an embarrassment later on when a communitarian, solidaristic ethos needs to be stressed.

*With regard to economic development, I stressed the possibilities and advantages of sequential problem-solving ("unbalanced growth") in *The Strategy of Economic Development* (New Haven: Yale University Press, 1958). Here I am rather concerned over the danger of getting stuck that comes with the availability of sequential solutions. The relation between these two positions is explored in my article "The Case Against 'One Thing at a Time,'" *World Development* 18 (August 1990): 1119–22.

Perhaps this is the basic reason why social welfare policies were pioneered by Bismarck's Germany, a country singularly unencumbered by a strong liberal tradition. Similarly, the more recent rhetorical assault against the Welfare State in the West has not been nearly as vigorous and sustained in Continental Western Europe as in England and the United States. None of this implies that in countries *with* a strong liberal tradition it is impossible to establish a comprehensive set of social welfare policies. But it is here that their introduction appears to require the concurrence of exceptional circumstances, such as the pressures created by depression or war, as well as special feats of social, political, and ideological engineering. Moreover, once introduced, Welfare State provisions will again come under attack at the first opportunity. The tension between the liberal tradition and the new solidarity ethos will remain unresolved for a long time, and the jeopardy thesis will be invoked with predictable regularity and will always find a receptive audience.

The Three Theses Compared and Combined

My main job is done. I have demonstrated how three distinct types of critiques, the perversity, futility, and jeopardy arguments, have been leveled unfailingly, if in multiple variants, at three major "revolutionary," "progressive," or "reform" moves of the last two hundred years. A synopsis in the form of a table will be useful.

A Synoptic Table

The table follows the order adopted in my text, except that "jeopardy" precedes "perversity" and "futility" instead of following them. In the table it is convenient for time to flow forward from left to right and from the top down. There is no doubt how to order the horizontal direction: as in the text, Marshall's three extensions of the concept of citizenship are listed in their "normal" historical order (the order, that is, in which they appeared in England): from the civil to the political to the socioeconomic aspect of citizenship. What is, on the other hand, the appropriate temporal order in the vertical direction depends on the sequence in which the three reactionary arguments have tended to make their appearance. There is reason to think, first of all, that jeopardy will generally be invoked ahead of perversity. The case for jeopardy can be made as soon as a new policy is proposed or officially adopted, whereas the perversity argument will normally arise only after some unhappy experiences with the new policy have accumulated. As to the futility argument, it is likely to make an even tardier appearance: as was pointed out early in Chapter 3, it takes some distance from the events for anyone to affirm that a great social movement was nothing but—much ado about nothing. Hence the "logical," perhaps the most likely time sequence for the diverse arguments to appear in relation to any one reform movement is jeopardy—perversity—futility. Various circumstances may of course make for departures from this pattern, as will be noted shortly.

The table recapitulates how the positions of major "reactionary" spokesmen have been accounted for and how they can be fitted into the intellectual scheme that has been laid out. It would no doubt be foolhardy on my part to claim exhaustiveness. I may well have overlooked an important figure here or a substantial argument there, precisely because neither fitted into my scheme.* But at this stage I feel rather more confident about having achieved tolerably comprehensive coverage than when I set out and declared (somewhat in jest, of course) that I

---

*It is not "preconceived," an adjective that is often—and often correctly—used in conjunction with the term "scheme." I formulated my three theses *after* having steeped myself for over a year in Burke, Maistre, Le Bon, Mosca, Hayek, Murray, and others. To be sure, once I had fastened onto my triad, further readings served primarily to confirm the scheme, which then probably assumed its usual role of shutting off its author from other possible insights.

Major exponents of three "reactionary" arguments during three historic epochs

Argument	Epoch		
	French Revolution / Rise of individual liberties	Universal suffrage / Rise of democracy	Rise of welfare state
Jeopardy	—	George Canning Robert Lowe Sir Henry Maine Fustel de Coulanges Max Scheler	Friedrich A. Hayek Samuel P. Huntington
Perversity	Edmund Burke Joseph de Maistre Adam Müller	Gustave Le Bon Herbert Spencer	Opponents of Poor Laws Advocates of New Poor Law Jay W. Forrester Nathan Glazer Charles Murray
Futility	Alexis de Tocqueville	Gaetano Mosca Vilfredo Pareto James Fitzjames Stephen	George Stigler Martin Feldstein Gordon Tullock

was limiting myself to three arguments purely for the sake of symmetry with the three episodes I was going to examine.

The three categories of perversity, futility, and jeopardy are in effect more exhaustive than meets the eye. When a public policy or "reform" is undertaken and then runs into problems or is viewed as a failure by some critics, this negative appraisal can in fact be attributed to only two basic reasons:

(1) The reform is viewed as not having accomplished its mission—perversity and futility are two stylized versions of this turn of events;

(2) The costs that are incurred and the consequences that are set off by the reform are considered to outweigh the benefits—a good portion of this (vast) territory is covered by the jeopardy argument, as was pointed out at the beginning of Chapter 4.

In other words, the three theses can after all be expected to account for the bulk of the rhetorical assaults I have undertaken to analyze.

The table bears witness to that fact. It is the ultimate reward for my effort to bring order to the diffuse world of reactionary rhetoric, and to show how that rhetoric reproduces itself from one episode to the next. I confess receiving considerable and intimate satisfaction from contemplating the table. Happily it has other uses as well: it stimulates and facilitates inquiry into a number of interactions and interrelations among the various points of view that have been discussed, up to now largely in isolation from one another.

To explore these interactions is the principal task of the following pages. Thus far the table has been explicated in the horizontal direction with each thesis being pursued through the three episodes in an attempt to understand its varieties, evolution, and nature. Since the table can also be read in the vertical direction, it is tempting to focus now on each of the progressive thrusts or episodes in the light of the very different critiques that have come forward. When this is done, a series of simple questions arises: Which argument has carried the most weight during each episode, and eventually overall? To what extent have the various arguments undercut one another or, on the contrary, when have they been mutually supportive? What has been the actual, as distinct from the "logical," time sequence with which the arguments have made their appearance? These questions have already come up occasionally in the course of the previous chapters, but a more systematic, though quite brief, presentation will be attempted here.

The Comparative Influence of the Theses

Take first the question about the comparative weights or influences to be attributed to the various theses. Answers can only be based on highly subjective judgments, and mine are implicit in my previous treatment. In recalling them I start with the most recent episode, involving the attack on what was once public provision for the poor and is now known as the Welfare State. The most influential argument here has been the claim that assistance to the poor merely serves to generate more poverty—the charge of perversity. Interestingly, it is the oldest as well as the most recent line of attack, involving Mandeville and Defoe all the way to the recent best-selling volume of Charles

Murray. A valuable auxiliary, but certainly subsidiary, role has been played by the futility claim, which asserts that large portions of the funds ostensibly destined to relieve poverty actually find their way to the pockets of the middle class.

Surprisingly, the least effective argument against the Welfare State has probably been the jeopardy thesis, which claims that welfare-state arrangements constitute a danger to individual liberties and to a properly functioning democratic society. In the more solidly established Western democracies this argument has lacked credibility, except in some periods—such as the seventies—when democratic institutions in several major countries appeared to be traversing a converging crisis.

Does the perverse effect occupy a similarly prominent position in the other two episodes? This is very much the case with regard to the French Revolution and the proclamation of the Rights of Man. Largely because of the spectacular dynamics of the Revolution, the idea that radical attempts at remaking society are bound to backfire has ever since been deeply ingrained in the collective unconscious. Tocqueville's demonstration that the Revolution did not wreak nearly as much change as it itself proclaimed (and has ordinarily been given credit for) and, correspondingly, his assertion that a number of significant social and political changes were already taking place under the Monarchy was a much more subtle way of undermining the Revolution's prestige and popularity. His speculations are fascinating for the modern social and economic historian, if only because he posed the "counterfactual" question whether France would have become a modern nation *without* the Revolution. Yet his work has only lately achieved the recognition it deserves, and even today the Revolution continues to be discussed mainly (and tiresomely) in traditional Manichean terms, with little attention to the questions raised by Tocqueville.

Finally, the jeopardy argument was never fully laid out for the French Revolution and the reason is simple: the revolutionary events came with such speed and swept away preexisting structures with such thoroughness that there was literally no time to determine whether there was something worth saving in the Ancien Régime.

Herein lies a basic difference from the episode that remains to be discussed. In the drive to universal suffrage and democratic governance during the nineteenth century, the comparative weight of the three arguments is very different. The basic discussion turned for a long time on the alleged incompatibility of democracy with liberty and on the fear that new political rights would damage past achievements, as illustrated by the debates around the two reform bills of 1832 and 1867 in England. More generally, real or imagined concerns about the "tyranny of the majority" kept the jeopardy argument alive even after the battle for universal suffrage had been decisively won. The perversity thesis, on the other hand, does not occupy a particularly prominent place in the attacks on democracy. Le Bon's argument about democracy's turning into tyrannical bureaucracy had considerably less bite than Mosca's and Pareto's attack on democracy as a sham and a screen for plutocracy and for a new kind of elite rule. In other words, the futility thesis did play a major role in the discussion alongside the jeopardy argument. It weakened support for democracy mainly in those countries— Italy and Germany, but also France—where individual liberties were not securely established before the advent of the suffrage and where the jeopardy argument was therefore not particularly applicable or persuasive.

In sum, each of the three theses has its own domain of special influence. To go further and establish an overall ranking among them in terms of historical importance is not a particularly meaningful exercise. If one were to go through with it, the perversity claim would probably be pronounced the "winner" as the single most popular and effective weapon in the annals of reactionary rhetoric.

The preceding argument has compared the political influence of the three theses. If they were to be judged instead in terms of intellectual merit, acuity, or sophistication, the rankings would probably be quite different. In the preceding text I have occasionally engaged in such comparisons, as when I said that the futility thesis makes for a more insulting critique of reform than the perversity thesis. But I see little point in holding a formal beauty, intelligence, or maliciousness contest.

Some Simple Interactions

The next issue to be explored with some help from the synoptic table is that of the mutual compatibility of the different arguments. The principal focus should again be on the columns rather than on the rows of the table: it is clearly of interest whether, as one of the three arguments is leveled against, say, the Welfare State, it is bolstered or undercut (or unaffected) by simultaneous or prior use of either of the other two arguments. But first let me briefly examine the rows with a similar question in mind: To what extent is each argument strengthened or weakened by the fact that a similar argument has already been used during a previous policy episode? The answers should be apparent from the first three chapters, which have followed the table along its horizontal dimensions by telling the story of the successive incarnations of each of the three theses in turn.

The extent to which the presentation of a given argument during one historical episode is helpful to the same argument as it is deployed during a subsequent phase will largely depend on the prestige the argument has gathered as a result of its earlier use. The perverse effect, for example, was formulated and extensively elaborated in the wake of the French Revolution, as shown in Chapter 2. The spectacular and commanding nature of the events from which the perverse effect was distilled endowed the principle with considerable authority and it came to be applied to a large number of subsequent policy-making episodes, from the extension of the franchise (Le Bon) to the building of low-cost houses (Forrester) to the compulsory use of seat belts (Peltzman). But here the perversity argument often did much less well, as the circumstances of policy-making were vastly different from those prevailing during the Revolution.

This experience provides successive illustrations for two contradictory maxims. At first, with the perversity thesis being applied to a wide array of policy experiences, it looks as though "nothing succeeds like success." But eventually, as the mechanical application of the thesis makes for increasingly less satisfactory accounts of reality, it appears rather that "nothing fails like success"—from a fresh insight the perversity claim turns into a knee-jerk response that blocks understanding. One is reminded of Marx's famous remark, in the *Eighteenth Brumaire of Louis Bonaparte,* that when history repeats itself that which first takes on the shape of tragedy will next time around appear as farce.[1] The implication is here precisely a dual one: (1) the second event owes a great deal to the ground's having been broken by the first, and (2) its imitative, derivative, and epigonic character is responsible for its "farcical" nature. This regularity is perhaps more likely to be reliably encountered in the history of ideas than in the history of events. It is well displayed in our stories, for example by the way Director's Law, as put forward by George Stigler, descends, in more than one meaning of this term, from Pareto's Law, which did have a genuine claim to being taken seriously as a scientific proposition.*

So much for situations where a thesis has achieved prestige as a result of its first appearance and encounter with social reality. What happens, in contrast, when a "reactionary" thesis does not fare particularly well when first asserted? An example is the jeopardy thesis, which was affirmed vigorously during the discussions around the English reform bills of 1832 and 1867. The bills were passed and the widely announced disaster—the Death of Liberty in England—did not happen. As a result, one

---

*This is the second time I find a well-known generalization or aphorism about the history of *events* to be more nearly correct when applied to the history of *ideas*. The first time was with regard to Santayana's famous dictum that those who do not learn from history are condemned to repeat it. Generalizing on the firm basis of this sample of two, I am tempted to formulate a "metalaw": historical "laws" that are supposed to provide insights into the history of events come truly into their own in the history of ideas. I give some reasons why this should be so when referring to the Santayana aphorism in *The Passions and the Interests* (Princeton: Princeton University Press, 1986), p. 133.

would expect the jeopardy argument to be a bit discredited for a while, and this seems indeed to have been the case, for the argument was not used to any substantial extent during the debate on the next reform bill in 1884. A "decent interval" was necessary for the argument to be invoked once again—almost eighty years separate Robert Lowe's solemn warnings about the imminent loss of liberty during the 1866 discussions on the Second Reform Bill from Hayek's similar alarm soundings in *The Road to Serfdom* (1944).

I now turn to what should be the more interesting interactions: those that take place along the *columns*, rather than the rows, of the table, among *different* arguments. The most striking instance of such interactions, the logical incompatibility and yet the mutual attraction of the perversity and futility arguments, has already been discussed at length in Chapter 3. Only a general point remains to be made: logical incompatibility between two arguments that are attacking the same policy or reform does not mean that they will not both be used in the course of some debate, sometimes even by the same person or group.

The two other pairs of arguments, jeopardy-perversity and jeopardy-futility, are tolerably compatible and could easily and perhaps effectively be marshalled together in combating some "progressive" move. It is then a matter of some surprise that such combinations do not occur with any frequency or regularity, at least as far as my survey indicates. Perhaps this is a result of the already noted point on temporal sequence: the jeopardy argument is apt to be voiced quite some time ahead of the other two. Thus Hayek's and then Huntington's jeopardy-type arguments against the Welfare State preceded the more recent Murray onslaught, which was entirely based on the perversity claim.

There are other explanations for the apparent failure to invoke jointly two arguments that are compatible and could be combined by the critics of some policy or reform. Advocates of one or the other of these arguments may simply have their hands full making their case along the lines of either jeopardy or perversity-futility. They may feel, moreover, that they would weaken rather than strengthen their case by appealing to too many arguments—just as a suspect must stay away from invoking too many alibis.

Our brief discussion yields an interesting paradox: when two arguments are nicely compatible, they are unlikely to be marshalled in conjunction. When they are incompatible, to the contrary, they may well both be used—perhaps because of the difficulty, the challenge, and the sheer outrageousness of it all.

A More Complex Interaction

Thus far my inquiry has been confined to the interactions within the individual rows of the table (for example, the perversity argument of Maistre with regard to the French Revolution was compared to that of Forrester with regard to the Welfare State) or to those within each column (for the discussions around the Welfare State, the perversity argument of Charles Murray was set against Stigler's futility argument). I now wish to examine the question, Is it conceivable for an argument put forward during one episode to affect the way *another* argument is deployed during a *different* episode? Or, in terms of the table, are there interesting interactions between cells belonging to different rows *and* columns?

Before focusing on one such case, I wish to recall briefly the rather unusual interaction within the same column that was encountered in Chapter 4. Toward the end of my discussion of the 1867 Reform Bill, I pointed out that the jeopardy argument against the extension of the franchise—the argument, that is, that universal suffrage would mean the end of "Liberty"—was undermined by a widespread feeling among the ruling elites that nothing much would change in English politics if the Reform Bill came to be enacted. There even were those—Disraeli among them—who thought that the expanded electorate would tilt politics in the *conservative* direction. In other words, the danger of jeopardy, as invoked by Robert Lowe, was not taken seriously by a number of actors, because they were already under the influence of the futility thesis and its argument that the much-heralded and much-feared advent of "democracy" was likely to be a nonevent. As noted in Chapter 3, James Fitzjames Stephen expressed this feeling in 1873, thus anticipating the Italian fin-de-siècle elite theorists and their more systematic deployment of the futility thesis.

From the formal point of view, one interesting feature of this interaction between jeopardy and futility is that jointly the two arguments, instead of lending mutual support in their respective attacks on suffrage, undercut each other: the futility thesis, which shows democracy to be largely a sham, makes it impossible to take seriously the jeopardy thesis, which sees democracy as a terrifying threat to "Liberty."

A similar result is obtained if we focus now on the

interaction between the same futility thesis—the one that scoffs at democracy—and the *next* jeopardy thesis, which portrays the Welfare State as a threat to democracy and liberty. It is easy to see how, once again, the futility argument will sabotage attempts at proclaiming jeopardy. This situation is particularly visible in Continental Europe, where Marshall's second and third phases (establishment of universal suffrage and welfare-state buildup) over-lapped to a considerable extent. In other words, the ideological assault on democracy was in full swing when the first important social insurance and social welfare measures were introduced. Under the circumstances it was against the grain for "reactionaries," who were in basic agreement with the arguments against democracy, to argue against the emerging welfare state along the lines of the jeopardy thesis, when that thesis typically extols democracy and warns about the dangers democracy would be exposed to from the welfare state.

Earlier I suggested that in some countries such as Germany the emergence of the welfare state was facilitated by the fact that the jeopardy argument could not be strongly articulated as long as neither individual liberties nor democratic political forms were extant or had been consolidated by the time the first social welfare measures were introduced. The point can now be strengthened. Even though democratic forms of government were already in existence, the jeopardy thesis may not have been invoked in some countries against welfare-state proposals because democracy never enjoyed uncontested prestige there, given the contemporary attacks against it on perversity and particularly futility grounds. In this way one reactionary argument (futility), put forward in the discussion around democracy, undercuts or impedes the use of another (jeopardy) during the virtually simultaneous debate about the welfare state. Ironically, such a constellation may facilitate the emergence of a new reform. It is notable that in Germany the welfare state, which took its vigorous first steps as early as the 1880s with Bismarck's social insurance laws, encountered determined critics along jeopardy lines only toward the middle of the twentieth century, with neoliberal figures such as Hayek and Wilhelm Röpke.

So far it looks as though the interaction between the futility argument of one episode (consolidation of democracy) and the jeopardy argument of the next (establishment of the welfare state) has been remarkably benign. The acceptance by part of public opinion of the futility argument directed against democracy can stave off the powerful opposition to the welfare state that might have been based on the jeopardy argument. But this very ideological constellation also harbors a quite different dynamic. The futility argument against democracy may produce not just the nonarticulation of the jeopardy thesis when social progress is on the agenda, but the active articulation of an argument that is the *inverse* of the jeopardy thesis: if there is conflict between democracy and social progress, let us press ahead with social progress, no matter what happens in the process to democracy, *which is a sham and a snare anyway!* With the exception of the Gorbachev turn, this has of course long been the Communist position—ever since Lenin's enthusiastic endorsement of the "dictatorship of the proletariat" in his 1917 pamphlet, *State and Revolution.*

That phrase goes back, to be sure, to Marx and to his

"Critique of the Gotha Program" of 1875, but it was really Lenin who gave it prominence and made allegiance to it into a test of Bolshevik orthodoxy. In doing so he was probably influenced not just by Marx, but by the discredit that was cast on "plutocratic" or "bourgeois" or "formal" democracy by prestigious contemporaries, such as Georges Sorel, Pareto, Michels, and numerous other detractors of democracy and practitioners of the futility argument.*

The interaction between the futility argument as directed against democracy and the jeopardy thesis in its various forms (including its inverse) has therefore been profoundly ambivalent: it has facilitated the emergence of the welfare state in some countries; in others, it has contributed to the belief that the loss or forgoing of democracy is an insignificant price to pay for social progress.

*There has been a long debate over the origins of Lenin's thought, and Lenin himself set the terms for it by proclaiming himself to be a faithful and strict follower of Marx. Those who refused to take his word for it then tried to show that, unbeknownst to himself, he was actually beholden to other, more remote yet powerful intellectual traditions. As Nicolas Berdyaev put it, for example, in *The Origins of Russian Communism* (New York: Scribner's, 1937), Russian communism is nothing but a "transformation and deformation of the old Russian messianic idea" (p. 228). See also David W. Lovell, *From Marx to Lenin* (Cambridge: Cambridge University Press, 1984), pp. 12–14. With the debate evolving between these two poles, both pointing to influences from the past, a third possibility has been totally neglected: Lenin, who for many years lived in Switzerland and elsewhere in Western Europe, may well have been influenced by the *contemporary* European intellectual atmosphere, with its virulent and visceral hostility toward democracy. That atmosphere, exemplified by the writings of Pareto, Sorel, and many others, has often been held responsible for the rise of fascism. It probably deserves broader credit.

From Reactionary to Progressive Rhetoric

"Reactionaries" have no monopoly on simplistic, peremptory, and intransigent rhetoric. Their "progressive" counterparts are likely to do just as well in this regard, and a book similar to the present one could probably be written about the principal arguments and rhetorical positions these folks have taken up over the last two centuries or so in making *their* case. That is not the book I set out to write, but chances are that a good deal of the repertoire of progressive or liberal rhetoric can be *generated* from the various reactionary theses here spelled out by turning them around, standing them on their head, or similar tricks. I shall now attempt to garner this sort of windfall profit from my previous search.

The Synergy Illusion and the Imminent-Danger Thesis

The success of the operation is likely to vary from one thesis to the other. Most promise seems to be held out by the jeopardy thesis, whose aptitude for metamorphism has already become manifest, both earlier in Chapter 4, where I showed it to be the opposite of an argument demonstrating how two successive reforms lend strength to each other, and again in the last few pages where a specific form of jeopardy claim was suddenly transmuted into an argument in favor of the dictatorship of the proletariat. But this transmutation was based on a complete reversal of underlying values. The premise of the jeopardy argument, as used to impugn welfare-state provisions, is the high value attributed to Liberty and Democracy. As long as this value prevails, any cogent argument to the effect that Liberty or Democracy is endangered by some newly proposed social or economic reform is likely to carry much weight. Once basic values change radically (in consequence, say, of the corrosive critique of Democracy delivered by the futility thesis), it is hardly surprising that the concern over jeopardy should be superseded by something very different—in the event, advocacy of the dictatorship of the proletariat for the purpose of achieving radical social change.

This advocacy is then the mirror image of the jeopardy thesis: the common assumption of both positions is the incompatibility of Liberty and Democracy, on the one hand, and of some social advance, on the other. The advocates of the jeopardy thesis feel that the social advance should be given up to preserve Liberty, whereas the partisans of the dictatorship of the proletariat make the opposite choice.

A very different transformation of the jeopardy thesis results when the assumption of *incompatibility* is given up and is replaced by the more cheerful idea, not only of compatibility, but of mutual support.

The ensuing antithesis of the jeopardy thesis was discussed at some length in Chapter 4. Whereas advocates of the jeopardy thesis seek out every conceivable conflict between a newly proposed reform and earlier improvements or achievements, it was shown there how progressive observers will focus on reasons why a new and an older reform will interact positively rather than negatively. A propensity to argue in favor of that sort of happy, positive interaction or *mutual support,* as I shall call it, is one of the hallmarks of the progressive temper. Progressives are eternally convinced that "all good things go together,"* in contrast to the zero-sum, *ceci-tuera-cela* mentality of the reactionaries. Beneath their different mentalities progressives and reactionaries do of course often hold quite different values. But, as we know, reactionaries frequently argue as though they were in basic agreement with the lofty objectives of the progressives; they "simply" point out that "unfortunately" things are not likely to go as smoothly as is taken for granted by their "naive" adversaries.

The jeopardy and the mutual support claims were shown to be "two limiting and equally unrealistic cases" of the many ways in which a new reform is likely to interact with an older one. Reactionaries exaggerate the harm to the older reform that will come from any new action or intervention, whereas progressives are excessively confident that all reforms are mutually supportive through

---

*The role of this concept in liberal thinking on economic and political development is emphasized in Robert A. Packenham, *Liberal America and the Third World* (Princeton: Princeton University Press, 1973). It is of course an ancient idea, traceable in particular to the Greeks, that there is harmony among, and even identity of, various desirable qualities such as the good, the beautiful, and the true. A celebrated expression of the idea is in Keats's "Ode on a Grecian Urn": "Beauty is truth, truth beauty."

what they like to call the principle of synergy. One might in fact designate the tendency of progressives to exaggerate along such lines as the "synergy illusion."

Not that progressives would never advert to any problems. But they typically perceive the dangers of *inaction,* rather than those of action. Here appears the outline of yet another transformation of the jeopardy thesis. The jeopardy argument stresses the dangers of action and the threat to past accomplishments that action carries. An opposite way of worrying about the future would be to perceive all kinds of approaching threats and dangers, and to advocate forceful *action* to forestall them.

For example, in pleading for the Reform Bill of 1867, Leslie Stephen argued that in the absence of reform the masses would resort to types of protest infinitely more threatening to established society than the vote. As was noted in Chapter 4, he saw the vote as a means to direct popular energies into comparatively innocuous channels and to delegitimize the more dangerous forms of popular protest such as strikes and riots.[1] Thus the jeopardy thesis was neatly turned around: it was the *failure* to enact the Reform Bill rather than its passage that was presented as being perilous to law, order, and liberty.

Similarly, the threats of social dissolution or of radicalization of the masses have often been cited as compelling arguments for instituting welfare-state provisions. In the area of international redistribution of income and wealth, the "imminent" threat of communism has been frequently invoked since World War II to clinch the case for transferring resources from the wealthier to the poorer countries. In all these situations the advocates of a certain policy felt that it was not good enough to argue for it on the ground that it was *right;* for greater rhetorical effect they urged that the policy was imperatively needed to stave off some threatening disaster.

This argument, which might be called the *imminent-danger thesis,** has two essential characteristics in common with its opposite, the jeopardy thesis. First of all, both look at only one category of dangers or risks when a new program is discussed: the jeopardy camp will conjure up exclusively the dangers of action, whereas the imminent-danger partisans will wholly concentrate on the risks of inaction.† Second, both camps present their respective scenarios—the harm that will come from either action or inaction—as though they were entirely certain and inescapable.

From these common exaggerations and illusions of reactionary *and* progressive rhetoric it is possible to derive, in contrast to both, two ingredients of what might be called a "mature" position:

(1) There are dangers and risks in both action and inaction. The risks of both should be canvassed, assessed, and guarded against to the extent possible.

(2) The baneful consequences of either action or inac-

---

*In a related context I have previously written about the "action-arousing gloomy vision." See *A Bias for Hope: Essays on Development and Latin America* (New Haven: Yale University Press, 1971), pp. 284, 350-353.

†Posing as a conservative obsessed by the dangers of action, Cornford nicely ironizes about the cavalier way such a person is apt to dismiss the opposite danger: "It is a mere theorist's paradox that doing nothing has just as many consequences as doing something. It is obvious that inaction can have no consequences at all." *Microcosmographia Academica* (Cambridge: Bowes & Bowes, 2nd ed., 1922), p. 29.

tion can never be known with the certainty affected by the two types of alarm-sounding Cassandras with whom we have become acquainted. When it comes to forecasts of impending mishaps or disasters, it is well to remember the saying *Le pire n'est pas toujours sûr*—the worst is not always sure (to happen).*

"Having History on One's Side"

The transformations of the jeopardy thesis have yielded two typical "progressive" positions: the synergistic fallacy about the ever-harmonious and mutually supportive relation between new and older reforms, and the imminent-danger argument about the need for proceeding apace with new reforms because of the dangers threatening in their absence.

Proceeding backward through our preceding text, it is now the turn of the futility thesis to generate a corresponding progressive stance. The essence of that thesis was the assertion that certain human attempts to effect change are destined to fail utterly because they run up against what Burke called the "eternal constitution of things" or, in nineteenth-century language, against "laws" or, still better, "iron laws" that rule the social world and simply cannot be tampered with: in our survey, authors

---

*This expression is the subtitle of Paul Claudel's play, *Le soulier de satin,* where it served to assert the possibility of salvation in as understated a form as possible. Claudel no doubt took it from the Spanish *No siempre lo peor es cierto,* the title of a comedy by Calderón de la Barca. The phrase is by now rather widely used in France—it has become "pro-verbialized."

or discoverers of such laws range from Pareto to Michels to Stigler-Director.

The so-called laws that buttress the futility thesis have a common characteristic: they uncover some previously hidden regularity that "rules" the social world and imparts *stability* to it. Such laws seem to be made-to-order to foil those who want to change the existing order. What about uncovering other types of laws that support the desire for change? These would be laws of *motion* that would give progressive social scientists the welcome assurance that the world is "irrevocably" moving in some direction they advocate.

The history of social science could actually be written in terms of the history of the search for these two kinds of laws. Here a thumbnail sketch must suffice.

Ever since the natural sciences came forward with laws ruling the physical universe, thinkers on human society have set out to discover general laws that govern the social world. What economists, for once under the influence of Freud, have lately taken to calling the "physics envy" of their discipline has long been a characteristic of all the social sciences. The aspiration found early expression in the assertion that the concept of "interest" provides a unified key to the understanding and prediction of human and social behavior. This conviction was already widespread in the seventeenth century and carried over into the eighteenth, as Helvétius wrote triumphantly, "As the physical universe is ruled by the laws of motion so is the moral universe ruled by laws of interest."[2]

The interest paradigm found its most elaborate and fruitful application in the building up of the new science of economics. Here it was used both for elucidating virtually timeless principles underlying the basic economic processes of exchange, production, consumption, and distribution *and* for understanding the specific economic and social changes that were visibly at work during the second half of the eighteenth century. The two endeavors coexisted peacefully for a while. For example, in Adam Smith's *Wealth of Nations* the historically oriented book 3 on the "Different Progress of Opulence in Different Nations" followed smoothly upon the first two books, whose broad analysis of economic processes, while never wholly abstract, was far less time-bound.

Then, in the nineteenth century, a certain division of labor set in among the law-pursuing social scientists. With economic and social change becoming increasingly spectacular in Western Europe, some specialized, as it were, in finding laws for these dynamic processes. Perhaps they were encouraged and lured into the undertaking by the exceptionally prestigious place Newton's mechanics had long occupied in the natural sciences. Helvétius for one obviously referred to these "laws of motion" and singled them out as though they were the only ones among the scientific accomplishments of the age that were worthy of notice in general and of emulation by thinkers about the "moral universe" in particular. A century later his call was heeded. It was Karl Marx's proudest claim—and he made it at his proudest moment, in the preface to *Capital*—that he had indeed "come upon the traces" of what he would call precisely "the economic law of motion [*Bewegungsgesetz*] of modern society," thereby all but designating himself the Newton of the social sciences.

Reactions to this claim were soon to set in. It has often been shown how, in the second half of the nineteenth century, the discovery by Jevons, Menger, and Walras of marginalism as a new foundation for economic analysis along quite general physio-psychological human-nature lines can be viewed as a response to Marx's endeavor to relativize economic knowledge, to restrict the validity of any set of economic "laws" to one particular "stage" of the "relations of production." Another onslaught on the Marxian claim to have discovered the "laws of motion" of contemporary society came with Mosca and Pareto and their assertion that there were certain "deep" economic and social structures (distribution of income and power) that were far more invariant than Marx had ever realized. This claim turned the tables on the Marxists: suddenly *they* were the shallow thinkers with their naive, Enlightenment-like belief in the malleability of society in the wake of "surface" events, be they reforms or even revolutions.

The purpose of the preceding short excursion into intellectual history will now have become clear. If the essence of the "reactionary" futility thesis is the natural-law–like *invariance* of certain socioeconomic phenomena, then its "progressive" counterpart is the assertion of *similarly lawlike* forward movement, motion, or *progress*. Marxism is simply the body of thought that has proclaimed with greatest aplomb the lawlike, inevitable character of a specific form of forward motion of human history. But numerous other doctrines have similarly claimed to have come upon the traces of one or another historical law of development. Any proposition to the effect that human societies pass necessarily through a finite and identical number of ascending *stages* is a close relative, on the progressive side, of what has here been described as the reactionary futility thesis.

The basic affinity between the two seemingly opposite theories is demonstrated by the way the language of futility is common to both. Marx is an excellent witness here. Immediately after having proclaimed his discovery of the "law of motion," he writes in his preface that modern society "cannot jump over the naturelike [*naturgemässe*] phases of development nor abolish them by decree." Futility, as exposed by the social scientist who has privileged knowledge about so-called laws of motion, consists here in the attempt to change or hinder their operation, whereas with Pareto and Stigler futility springs correspondingly from the vain effort to tamper with some basic *constant*.

It has been one of the more frequent objections to the Marxian system and to similar ideas of inevitable progress—for in this respect Marxism is but the heir of the Enlightenment—that they seem to leave little scope for human action. As long as the future transformation of bourgeois society is already certain, what point is there for you and me to actually put our shoulder to the wheel? Here is an early form of what became famous later as the "free rider" problem, and, as is true for that only slightly more sophisticated argument, it is not nearly as problematic as it sounds. Marx himself anticipated the argument by pointing out, again in the preface to *Capital*, that working for the "inevitable" revolution would help to accelerate its coming and to reduce its cost. More generally, people enjoy and feel empowered by the confidence, however vague, that they *"have history on their side."* This concept was a typical nineteenth-century successor to the earlier assurance, much sought after by all combatants, that *God* was on their side. Nobody ever suggested, as far as I am aware, that this assurance would weaken anyone's fighting spirit. Activism was similarly stimulated by the idea of the actors being backed by a historical law of motion, and this was indeed the intent of the proponents of that construction. For its reactionary counterpart, the futility argument, a corresponding story holds: if taken to heart, this argument does radically discourage human action, and this is once again exactly what *its* exponents set out to achieve.

Counterparts of the Perversity Thesis

For both the jeopardy and the futility theses the transformation of reactionary rhetoric into its opposite resulted in types (or stereotypes) of progressive rhetoric—from the synergy illusion to the belief in having history on one's side—that, while not wholly unfamiliar, nevertheless enrich our commonsense understanding of what this rhetoric is about. There is some question whether this feat can be repeated in the case of the perversity thesis. The perverse effect occupies so central a place in the world of reactionary rhetoric that its obverse is likely to take us right back to what everybody already knows about the typical progressive mentality. The point is best demonstrated in conjunction with various discourses on the paradigmatic progressive event of modern history, the French Revolution.

The reactionary position consists in proclaiming the widespread incidence of the perverse effect. Reactionaries therefore recommend extreme caution in reshaping existing institutions and in pursuing innovative policies. The progressive counterpart to this position is to throw that caution to the wind, to disregard not only tradition but the whole concept of unintended consequences of human action, whether or not it actually results in perversity: progressives are forever ready to mold and remold society at will and have no doubt about their ability to control events. This propensity to large-scale social engineering was in fact one of the striking features of the French Revolution. Hailed by the young Hegel as a "magnificent dawn," the Revolution's pretense at building a new social order in accordance with "rational" principles soon came to be denounced as disastrous by contemporary critics invoking the perversity argument. Later Tocqueville used a rather mocking tone as he likened the revolutionary undertaking to an attempt at molding reality in accordance with bookish schemes invented by the *gens de lettres* of the Enlightenment.

> When one studies the history of our revolution one sees that it was conducted in the same spirit that presides over many abstract books on the principles of government. Same attraction toward general theories, complete systems of legislation, and exact symmetry of laws; same contempt for existing facts; same trust in theory; same taste for what is original, ingenious, and novel in designing institutions; same bent for remaking simultaneously the entire constitution, following the rules of logic and a unique plan, instead of attempting to amend its parts. A frightening spectacle![3]

The assertion of the need to rebuild society from the ground up according to the dictates of "reason" (that is, in accordance with someone's idea of what "reason" commands) is then the thesis against which the perversity argument arose as the antithesis. But to a considerable and surprising extent, the thesis survived the antithesis. In fact, there has never been an adequate explanation of why utopian thought should have flourished as abundantly and extravagantly as it did in the nineteenth century *after* the searing experiences of the French Revolution and the ensuing explicit formulation of the perversity thesis.[4]

What actually happened was that the Burkean critique of the French Revolution led to an *escalation* of revolutionary and progressive rhetoric. An essential component of Burke's thought was his assertion, based primarily on the English historical experience, that existing institutions incorporated a great deal of collective evolutionary wisdom and that they were, moreover, quite capable of evolving gradually. If this fundamental conservative objection to radical change was to be overruled, it became necessary to argue that English history was very special and privileged, that there are countries which have no tradition of liberty whatever and where existing institutions are rotten through and through. Under such conditions there is no alternative to the demolition of the old combined with a comprehensive reconstruction of political society and economic order, no matter how hazardous such an undertaking may be in terms of unleashing perverse effects.

Burke was criticized along such lines as early as 1853 by the French liberal writer Charles de Rémusat:

If the events, in their fatality, have been such that a people does not find, or does not know how to find, its own entitlements [*titres*] in its annals, if no epoch of its history has left behind a good national memory,

161

then all the morals and all the archeology one can mobilize will not be able to endow that people with the faith it lacks nor with the attitudes this faith might have forged . . . If to be free a people must have been so in the past, if it must have had a good government to be able to aspire to one today or *if at least it must be able to imagine having had these two things,* then such a people is immobilized by its own past, its future is foreclosed; and there are nations that are condemned to dwell forever in despair.[5]

In this remarkable passage Rémusat says not only that there are situations and countries where the Burkean reverence for the past is totally out of place; of greater interest is his point that the validity of Burke's critique depends largely on the people's understanding and imaginings of its condition. In other words, the Burkean critique, with its assertion of the perverse effect, made it imperative for advocates of radical change to cultivate "the sense of being in a desperate predicament"[6] as well as what I called fracasomania (failure complex) in my earlier studies of policy-making in Latin America; that is, the conviction that all attempts at solving the nation's problems have ended in utter failure. Where such attitudes prevail, the Burkean insistence on the possibility of gradual change and on the perfectibility of existing institutions is effectively countered and deflected. By invoking the desperate predicament in which a people is caught, as well as the failure of prior attempts at reform, it is implicitly or explicitly argued that the old order must be smashed and a new one rebuilt from scratch *regardless* of any counterproductive consequences that might ensue. The invocation of the desperate predicament can therefore be seen as a rhetorical maneuver of escalation meant to neutralize and override the argument of the perverse effect.*

In searching for a nonobvious counterpart to the perversity argument, I have come upon a curious unintended consequence of Burke's conservative critique of the French Revolution. By insisting on the perfectibility of existing institutions as an argument against radical change, his *Reflections* may have contributed to a long line of radical writings that portray the situation of this or that country as being totally beyond repair, reform, or improvement.

This is the end of my digression into progressive rhetoric. Like its reactionary counterpart, it turns out to be richer in maneuvers, largely of exaggeration and obfuscation, than it is ordinarily given credit for.

*I do not wish to claim that the desperate-predicament argument was not used prior to the French Revolution. It would be hard to improve upon the following statement of Emmanuel Sieyès, at the end of his "Essai sur les privilèges" (1788): "A time will come when our outraged grandchildren will be appalled upon reading our history and when the most inconceivable madness [*la plus inconcevable démence*] will be called by its well-deserved names." In Sieyès, *Qu'est-ce que le Tiers Etat?* (Paris: Presses Universitaires de France, 1982), p. 24. My point is that the Burkean critique increased the likelihood and incidence of this sort of extremist pronouncement.

SEVEN

Beyond Intransigence

A Turnabout in Argument?

By turning, in the previous chapter, from "reactionaries" to "progressives" and to some of the typical arguments and debating points of the latter, I may have lost quite a few of whatever friends I made in the course of the first three chapters, which dissected and exposed various types of reactionary rhetoric. I hasten to reassure them by recalling briefly my main theme and endeavor. The predominant purpose of this book has been to trace some key reactive/reactionary theses through the debates of the last two hundred years and to demonstrate how the protagonists followed certain invariants in argument and rhetoric. To show how advocates of reactionary causes are caught by compelling reflexes and lumber predictably through set motions and maneuvers does not in itself refute the arguments, of course; but it does have a number of fairly corrosive consequences.

I shall start with a minor one. As a result of my procedure, some "deep thinkers" who had invariably presented their ideas as original and brilliant insights are made to look rather less impressive, and sometimes even comical.

That effect was initially unintended, but it is not unwelcome. There has been a certain lack of balance in the recurring debates between progressives and conservatives: in the effective use of the potent weapon of irony, conservatives have had a clear edge over progressives. Already Tocqueville's critique of the Revolutionary project, as put forth in the passage cited in Chapter 6, uses a sarcastic tone. In his hands that project begins to look naive and absurd, rather than infamous and sacrilegious—the predominant characterization conveyed by earlier critics such as Maistre and Bonald. This aspect of the conservatives' attitude toward their opponents was also reflected in the German term *Weltverbesserer* (world improver), which evokes someone who has taken on far too much and is bound to end up as a ridiculous failure. (The American term "do-gooder" has similar connotations of derision, but to a lesser degree, in that the projects of the do-gooder tend to be less grand than those of the *Weltverbesserer*.) In general, a skeptical, mocking attitude toward progressives' endeavors and likely achievements is an integral and highly effective component of the modern conservative stance.

In contrast, progressives have remained mired in earnestness. Most of them have been long on moral indignation and short on irony.* The present volume goes perhaps some way toward correcting this imbalance.

But that is hardly a sufficient justification for having labored on this book. There has indeed been a more basic intent: to establish some presumption, through the dem-

---

*An exception must obviously be made for the ever-witty F. M. Cornford.

onstration of repetition in basic argument, that the standard "reactionary" reasoning, as here exhibited, is frequently *faulty*. The fact that an argument is used repeatedly is no proof, to be sure, that it is wrong in any particular instance. I have said so here and there already, but it bears repeating quite bluntly and generally: there certainly have existed situations where well-intentioned "purposive social action" has had perverse effects, others where it has been essentially futile, and still others where it has jeopardized the benefits due to some preceding advance. My point is that, much of the time, the arguments I have identified and reviewed are intellectually *suspect* on several counts.

A general suspicion of overuse of the arguments is aroused by the demonstration that they are invoked time and again almost routinely to cover a wide variety of real situations. The suspicion is heightened when it can be shown, as I have attempted to do in the preceding pages, that the arguments have considerable intrinsic appeal because they hitch onto powerful myths (Hubris-Nemesis, Divine Providence, Oedipus) and influential interpretive formulas (*ceci tuera cela*, zero-sum) or because they cast a flattering light on their authors and provide a boost for their egos. In view of these extraneous attractions, it becomes likely that the standard reactionary theses will often be embraced regardless of their fit.

Far from diluting my message, the preceding chapter on progressive rhetoric further strengthens this point. By demonstrating that each of the reactionary arguments has one or more progressive counterparts, I generated contrasting *pairs* of reactionary and progressive statements about social action. To recall some of them:

166

Reactionary: The contemplated action will bring disastrous consequences.

Progressive: Not to take the contemplated action will
bring disastrous consequences.

Reactionary: The new reform will jeopardize the older
one.

Progressive: The new and the old reforms will mutually reinforce each other.

Reactionary: The contemplated action attempts to
change permanent structural characteristics ("laws") of the social order; it is therefore bound to be wholly ineffective, futile.

Progressive: The contemplated action is backed up by
powerful historical forces that are already
"on the march"; opposing them would be
utterly futile.

Once the existence of these pairs of arguments is demonstrated, the reactionary theses are downgraded, as it
were: they, along with their progressive counterparts, become simply extreme statements in a series of imaginary,
highly polarized debates. In this manner they stand effectively exposed as *limiting cases,* badly in need, under most
circumstances, of being qualified, mitigated, or otherwise
amended.

How *Not* to Argue in a Democracy

Having justified the usefulness of Chapter 6 from the very
point of view which presided over the original conception

of this book, I can now state that writing that chapter has made me visualize a broader role for the whole exercise. What I have ended up doing, in effect, has been to map the *rhetorics of intransigence* as they have long been practiced by both reactionaries and progressives.

Flaubert once employed a marvelous phrase to blast the opposing schools of philosophers that assert everything to be either pure matter or pure spirit: such affirmations, he said, are "two identical impertinences" (*deux impertinences égales*).[1] This term is also apt in characterizing the twin statements just formulated.

Yet my purpose is not to cast "a plague on both your houses." Rather, it is to move public discourse beyond extreme, intransigent postures of either kind, with the hope that in the process our debates will become more "democracy friendly."* This is a large topic and I cannot deal with it adequately here. A concluding thought must suffice.

Recent reflections on democracy have yielded two valuable insights, a historical one on the origins of pluralistic democracies and a theoretical one on the long-run conditions for stability and legitimacy of such regimes. Modern pluralistic regimes have typically come into being, it is increasingly recognized, not because of some preexisting wide consensus on "basic values," but rather because various groups that had been at each other's throats for a prolonged period had to recognize their mutual inability to achieve dominance. Tolerance and acceptance of pluralism resulted eventually from a *standoff* between bitterly hostile opposing groups.[2]

*A term coined in analogy to the now-common "user friendly" or to the German *umweltfreundlich* (environment friendly).

168

This historical point of departure of democracy does not bode particularly well for the stability of these regimes. The point is immediately obvious, but it becomes even more so when it is brought into contact with the theoretical claim that a democratic regime achieves legitimacy to the extent that its decisions result from full and open deliberation among its principal groups, bodies, and representatives. Deliberation is here conceived as an opinion-forming process: the participants should not have fully or definitively formed opinions at the outset; they are expected to engage in meaningful discussion, which means that they should be ready to modify initially held opinions in the light of arguments of other participants and also as a result of new information which becomes available in the course of the debate.[3]

If this is what it takes for the democratic process to become self-sustaining and to acquire long-run stability and legitimacy, then the gulf that separates such a state from democratic-pluralistic regimes as they emerge historically from strife and civil war is uncomfortably and perilously wide. A people that only yesterday was engaged in fratricidal struggles is not likely to settle down overnight to those constructive give-and-take deliberations. Far more likely, there will initially be agreement to disagree, but without any attempt at melding the opposing points of view—that is indeed the nature of religious tolerance. Or, if there is discussion, it will be a typical "dialogue of the deaf"—a dialogue that will in fact long function as a prolongation of, and a substitute for, civil war. Even in the most "advanced" democracies, many debates are, to paraphrase Clausewitz, a "continuation of civil war with other means." Such debates, with each party on the lookout for arguments that kill, are only too familiar from democratic politics as usual.

There remains then a long and difficult road to be traveled from the traditional internecine, intransigent discourse to a more "democracy-friendly" kind of dialogue. For those wishing to undertake this expedition there should be value in knowing about a few danger signals, such as arguments that are in effect contraptions specifically designed to make dialogue and deliberation impossible. I have here attempted to supply a systematic and historically informed account of these arguments on one side of the traditional divide between "progressives" and "conservatives"—and have then added, much more briefly, a similar account for the other side. As compared to my original aim of exposing the simplicities of reactionary rhetoric alone, I end up with a more even-handed contribution—one that could ultimately serve a more ambitious purpose.

Notes
Acknowledgments
Index

Notes

One. Two Hundred Years of Reactionary Rhetoric

1. The report of the group was later published as *The Common Good: Social Welfare and the American Future*, Policy Recommendations of the Executive Panel (New York: Ford Foundation, 1989).
2. T. H. Marshall, "Citizenship and Social Class," Alfred Marshall Lectures given at Cambridge University in 1949, reprinted in Marshall, *Class, Citizenship, and Social Development* (New York: Doubleday, 1965), chap. 4.
3. Alfred N. Whitehead, *Symbolism* (New York: Capricorn, reprint ed., 1959), p. 88.
4. A short list of relevant titles: François Bourricaud, *Le retour de la droite* (Paris: Calmann-Lévy, 1986); Jacques Godechot, *La contre-révolution* (Paris: Presses Universitaires de France, 1961); Russell Kirk, *The Conservative Mind, from Burke to Eliot* (Chicago: Regnery, 1960); Karl Mannheim, *Conservatism* (London: Routledge & Kegan Paul, 1986); Michael Oakeshott, *Rationalism in Politics, and Other Essays* (London: Methuen, 1962), particularly the title essay and "On Being Conservative"; Anthony Quinton, *The Politics of Imperfection* (London: Faber & Faber, 1978); Roger Scruton, *The Meaning of Conservatism* (London: Macmillan, 1980); and Peter Steinfels, *The Neoconservatives* (New York: Simon & Schuster, 1979).

5. See Jean Starobinski, "La vie et les aventures du mot 'réaction,'" *Modern Language Review* 70 (1975): xxii–xxxi; also Bronislaw Baczko, *Comment sortir de la terreur: Thermidor et la Révolution* (Paris: Gallimard, 1989), pp. 328–336.
6. Cited in Starobinski, "La vie du mot 'réaction,'" p. xxiii.
7. I. Bernard Cohen, "The Newtonian Scientific Revolution and Its Intellectual Significance," *Bulletin of the American Academy of Arts and Sciences* 41 (December 1987): 16.
8. Ferdinand Brunot, *Histoire de la langue française des origines à 1900* (Paris: A. Colin, 1922–1953), vol. 9, pt. 2, p. 844.
9. Benjamin Constant, *Ecrits et discours politiques*, ed. O. Pozzo di Borgo (Paris: Jean-Jacques Pauvert, 1964), vol. 1, pp. 84–85.

Two. The Perversity Thesis

1. For a broad survey of perverse effects by a sociologist, see Raymond Boudon, *Effets pervers et ordre social* (Paris: Presses Universitaires de France, 1977).
2. Edmund Burke, *Reflections on the Revolution in France*, ed. and intro. Conor Cruise O'Brien (Middlesex: Penguin Classics, 1986), pp. 313, 345.
3. Alfred Cobban, *Edmund Burke and the Revolt against the Eighteenth Century* (London: Allen & Unwin, 1929), p. 123.
4. Friedrich Schiller to Herzog Friedrich Christian von Augustenburg, July 13, 1793, in *Schiller's Briefe*, ed. Fritz Jonas (Stuttgart: Deutsche Verlagsanstalt, 1892–96), vol. 3, p. 333.
5. Adam Müller, *Schriften zur Staatsphilosophie*, ed. Rudolf Kohler (Munich: Theatiner-Verlag, 1923), p. 232. The passage is from Müller's 1819 essay, "Von der Notwendigkeit einer theologischen Grundlage der gesamten Staatswissenschaften und der Staatswirtschaft insbesondere" (On the need

for a theological basis for the social sciences and for political economy in particular); it is cited prominently in Carl Schmitt, *Politische Romantik*, 2nd ed. (Munich: Duncker & Humblot, 1925), p. 170.

6. By Conor Cruise O'Brien in his introduction to Burke, *Reflections*, pp. 70–73.

7. Burke, *Reflections*, pp. 138, 271.

8. *The Letters of Jacob Burckhardt*, ed. A. Dru (London: Routledge & Kegan Paul, 1955), p. 93.

9. Gustave Flaubert, *Correspondance* (Paris: Conard, 1930), vol. 6, pp. 282, 33, 228, 287.

10. Ibid., p. 287.

11. Henrik Ibsen, *An Enemy of the People*, act 4.

12. Herbert Dieckmann, "Diderot's Conception of Genius," *Journal of the History of Ideas* 2 (April 1941): 151–182.

13. Gustave Le Bon, *Psychologie des foules* (Paris: Félix Alcan, 1895), p. 4.

14. Ibid., p. 169.

15. Ibid., p. 187.

16. Herbert Spencer, *The Man versus the State* (Caldwell, Idaho: Caxton Printers, 1940), p. 86.

17. Milton Friedman, *Capitalism and Freedom* (Chicago: University of Chicago Press, 1962), p. 180.

18. Edward Bulwer-Lytton, *England and the English* (New York: Harper, 1833), vol. 1, p. 129. Part of this passage is cited in Gertrude Himmelfarb, *The Idea of Poverty: England in the Early Industrial Age* (New York: Knopf, 1984), p. 172.

19. Charles Murray, *Losing Ground: America's Social Policy, 1950–1980* (New York: Basic Books, 1984), p. 9.

20. This is Himmelfarb's summary of William Cobbett's repeated indictment of the New Poor Law in his tract, *A Legacy to Labourers* (London, 1834). See *The Idea of Poverty*, p. 211.

21. Quoted in Himmelfarb, *The Idea of Poverty*, p. 182.

22. See Nicholas C. Edsall, *The Anti–Poor Law Movement, 1834–44* (Manchester: Manchester University Press, 1971).

23. E. P. Thompson, *The Making of the English Working Class* (New York: Vintage, 1963), p. 267.
24. Jay W. Forrester, "Counterintuitive Behavior of Social Systems," *Technology Review* 73 (January 1971).
25. Nathan Glazer, "The Limits of Social Policy," *Commentary* 52 (September 1971).
26. For a noncatastrophic appraisal, see Mary Jo Bane, "Is the Welfare State Replacing the Family?" *Public Interest* 70 (Winter 1983): 91–101.
27. Joseph de Maistre, *Considérations sur la France*, ed. Jean-Louis Darcel (Geneva: Slatkine, 1980), p. 95.
28. Thomas Hobbes, *Leviathan*, II, chap. 30.
29. Anson Rabinbach, "Knowledge, Fatigue, and the Politics of Industrial Accidents," in *Social Knowledge and the Origins of Modern Social Policy*, ed. Dietrich Rueschemeyer and Theda Skocpol (forthcoming).
30. Fred Block and Frances Fox Piven, "The Contemporary Relief Debate," in Fred Block et al., *The Mean Season: The Attack on the Welfare State* (New York: Pantheon, 1987), p. 96.
31. Ibid., pp. 96–98.

Three. The Futility Thesis

1. Alphonse Karr, *Les guêpes*, new ed. (Paris: Calmann-Lévy, 1891), vol. 6, p. 305.
2. Giuseppe Tomasi di Lampedusa, *Il Gattopardo* (Milan: Feltrinelli, 1959), p. 42.
3. Edmund Burke, *Reflections on the Revolution in France*, ed. and intro. Conor Cruise O'Brien (Middlesex: Penguin Classics, 1986), p. 92.
4. Charles de Rémusat, "'L'Ancien Régime et la Révolution' par Alexis de Tocqueville," *Revue des deux mondes* 4 (1856): 656.
5. J. J. Ampère, *Mélanges d'histoire littéraire* (Paris, 1877), vol.

2, pp. 320–323. The passage here quoted is reproduced from a review written in 1856. See also Richard Herr, *Tocqueville and the Old Regime* (Princeton: Princeton University Press, 1962), pp. 108–109.

6. François Furet, *Penser la Révolution Française* (Paris: Gallimard, 1978), p. 31. Emphasis added.

7. Alexis de Tocqueville, *L'Ancien Régime et la Révolution*, 4th ed. (Paris, 1860), p. 333.

8. Gaetano Mosca, *The Ruling Class* (*Elementi di scienza politica*), ed. and intro. Arthur Livingston (New York: McGraw-Hill, 1939), p. x.

9. Ibid., pp. 284–285.

10. Gaetano Mosca, "Teorica dei governi e governo parlamentare," in *Scritti politici*, ed. Giorgio Sola (Turin: U.T.E.T., 1982), vol. 1, p. 476; translation adapted from James H. Meisel, *The Myth of the Ruling Class* (Ann Arbor: University of Michigan Press, 1958), p. 106. Emphasis in original.

11. Mosca, "Teorica," p. 478. Emphasis in original.

12. Richard Bellamy, *Modern Italian Social Theory* (Stanford: Stanford University Press, 1987), pp. 40–41.

13. Gaetano Mosca, *Il tramonto dello stato liberale*, ed. Antonio Lombardi (Catania: Bonanno, 1971), pp. 82–88, 123–141.

14. Vilfredo Pareto, *Cours d'économie politique*, ed. G. H. Bousquet and Giovanni Busino (Geneva: Droz, 1964), par. 1054.

15. Ibid., par. 1055.

16. Moisei Ostrogorski published his pathbreaking two-volume work, *La démocratie et les partis politiques* (Paris: Calmann-Lévy), in 1903. His findings on the American political system had been published as early as 1888–1889 in *Annales des sciences politiques,* and it is therefore quite possible that they had come to Pareto's attention by the time he wrote the *Cours.* In tracing the influence of Ostrogorski's work on contemporary social scientists, Seymour Martin Lipset gives that date of publication erroneously as the "early 1890s." See Lipset's otherwise highly instructive article, "Moisei Ostrogorski and the Analytical Approach to the Com-

parative Study of Political Parties" in Lipset, *Revolution and Counterrevolution* (New York: Basic Books, 1968), p. 366.

17. Pareto, *Cours*, par. 1056.

18. Vilfredo Pareto, "La courbe de la répartition de la richesse" (1896), republished in Pareto, *Ecrits sur la courbe de la répartition de la richesse*, ed. and intro. Giovanni Busino (Geneva: Droz, 1965), pp. 1–15; *Cours*, pars. 950–968.

19. Pareto, "La courbe," p. 3.

20. *Palgrave's Dictionary of Political Economy* (London: Macmillan, 1926 ed.).

21. First published in German with the title *Zur Soziologie des Parteiwesens in der modernen Demokratie* (Leipzig: Klinkhardt, 1911) and translated into English, with an introduction by Seymour Martin Lipset, as Robert Michels, *Political Parties* (New York: Free Press, 1962).

22. Pareto, *Cours*, par. 965.

23. Pareto, *Ecrits sur la courbe*, p. x.

24. Ibid., p. 17.

25. Lampedusa, *Il Gattopardo*, p. 219.

26. James Fitzjames Stephen, *Liberty, Equality, Fraternity*, ed. R. J. White (Cambridge: Cambridge University Press, 1967), p. 211. See also James A. Colaiaco, *James Fitzjames Stephen and the Crisis of Victorian Thought* (New York: St. Martin's Press, 1983), p. 154. James Fitzjames Stephen was the brother of the more liberal and better-known Leslie Stephen, who had contributed an eloquent article in favor of electoral reform to the 1867 *Essays on Reform*, republished in 1967 as *A Plea for Democracy*. See also Chapter 6, note 1.

27. Stephen, *Liberty, Equality, Fraternity*, p. 212.

28. George Stigler, "Director's Law of Public Income Distribution," *Journal of Law and Economics* 13 (April 1970): 1–10.

29. Milton Friedman and Rose Friedman, *Free to Choose* (New York: Avon Books, 1979), p. 109.

30. Gordon Tullock, *Welfare for the Well-to-Do* (Dallas: Fisher Institute, 1983).

31. Gordon Tullock, *Economics of Income Redistribution* (Hingham, Mass.: Kluwer Nijhoff, 1983).
32. Ibid., pp. 100–101.
33. Martin Feldstein, "Unemployment Compensation: Adverse Incentives and Distributional Anomalies," *National Tax Journal* 27 (June 1974): 231–244; quotation on p. 231.
34. Ibid., p. 237.
35. Martin Feldstein, "New Evidence on the Distribution of Unemployment Insurance Benefits," *National Tax Journal* 30 (June 1977): 219–222.
36. Feldstein, "Unemployment Compensation," p. 237.
37. Robert E. Goodin and Julian LeGrand, *Not Only the Poor: The Middle Classes and the Welfare State* (London: Allen & Unwin, 1987).
38. See Anne O. Krueger, "The Political Economy of the Rent-Seeking Society," *American Economic Review* 64 (May 1974): 291–303; and James M. Buchanan et al., eds., *Toward a Theory of the Rent-Seeking Society* (College Station: Texas A&M University Press, 1980).
39. See Albert O. Hirschman, "Ideology: Mask or Nessus Shirt?" in *Comparison of Economic Systems*, ed. Alexander Eckstein (Berkeley: University of California Press, 1971), p. 295.

Four. The Jeopardy Thesis

1. Isaiah Berlin, "Two Concepts of Liberty," reprinted in Berlin, *Four Essays on Liberty* (Oxford: Oxford University Press, 1969), chap. 3. Berlin mentions neither T. H. Marshall nor Benjamin Constant.
2. See Quentin Skinner, "The Paradoxes of Political Liberty," in *The Tanner Lectures on Human Values* (Salt Lake City: University of Utah Press, 1986), vol. 7, pp. 227–250. This fine paper contains extensive references to the literature.
3. Benjamin Constant, "De la liberté des Anciens comparée à

celle des Modernes," in Constant, *De la liberté chez les Modernes*, ed. Marcel Gauchet (Paris: Le Livre de Poche, 1980), pp. 491–518. Constant's distinction between the two concepts of liberty can be traced further back to Madame de Staël, to Emmanuel Sieyès, and even to Rousseau. See "Madame de Staël" (by Marcel Gauchet) in François Furet and Mona Ozouf, *Dictionnaire critique de la Révolution Française* (Paris: Flammarion, 1988), p. 1057; for Sieyès, see Pasquale Pasquino, "Emmanuel Sieyès, Benjamin Constant et le 'gouvernement des Modernes,'" *Revue française de Science Politique* 37 (April 1987): 214–228; Rousseau, whom Constant criticized for ignoring the distinction, was occasionally quite aware of it, for example, in his *Lettres écrites de la montagne*, as noted in my *Shifting Involvements* (Princeton: Princeton University Press, 1982), p. 98.

4. J. R. M. Butler, *The Passing of the Great Reform Bill* (New York: Augustus M. Kelley, 1965), pp. 240–241.

5. Ibid., p. 237.

6. Quoted in "The Real Character and Tendency of the Proposed Reform," anonymous pamphlet (London: Roake & Varty, 1831), p. 21.

7. Asa Briggs, *The Age of Improvement* (London: Longmans, Green, 1959), p. 258.

8. Quoted in Butler, *Reform Bill*, p. 257.

9. Thomas C. Schelling, *The Strategy of Conflict* (Cambridge, Mass.: Harvard University Press, 1960), p. 57.

10. F. B. Smith, *The Making of the Second Reform Bill* (Cambridge: Cambridge University Press, 1966), p. 233.

11. See Briggs, *Age of Improvement*, p. 513. The last chapter, on the Reform Bill of 1867, is entitled "The Leap in the Dark." The phrase has been traced back to Macaulay and to one of his speeches in favor of the 1832 Reform Bill, but it was made famous by Lord Derby in 1867. See Gertrude Himmelfarb, *Victorian Minds* (New York: Knopf, 1968), p. 383.

12. The Right Hon. Robert Lowe, M.P., *Speeches and Letters on Reform* (London, 1867), p. 170.

13. Ibid., p. 61.
14. *The Letters of Thomas Babbington Macaulay*, ed. Thomas Pinney (Cambridge: Cambridge University Press, 1981), vol. 6, p. 94. In this letter Macaulay anticipates the frontier thesis of Frederick Jackson Turner, according to which the American frontier acts as a safety valve for social conflict.
15. Ibid.
16. W. E. H. Lecky, *Democracy and Liberty* (London: Longmans, 1896), vol. 1, p. 18.
17. Lowe, *Speeches*, pp. 158, 161, 147ff.
18. Ibid., p. 149.
19. Sir Henry Sumner Maine, *Popular Government: Four Essays* (New York: Henry Holt, 1886), pp. 35–36.
20. Ibid., pp. 97–98. My emphasis.
21. Gustave Le Bon, *Psychologie des foules* (Paris: Félix Alcan, 1895), p. 44.
22. Quoted in Himmelfarb, *Victorian Minds*, p. 334.
23. Lowe, *Speeches*, p. 76.
24. *Quarterly Review* 127 (1869): 541–542, cited in Himmelfarb, *Victorian Minds*, pp. 357–358.
25. W. L. Guttsman, ed., *A Plea for Democracy*, pp. 72–92; and Hirschman, *Shifting Involvements*, pp. 115–116.
26. M. Prévost-Paradol, *Quelques pages d'histoire contemporaine*, ser. 4 (Paris: Michel Lévy, 1867), p. vi.
27. Fustel de Coulanges, *La cité antique* (Paris: Hachette, 1885), pp. 1–2. Emphasis added.
28. Ibid., p. 268.
29. Ibid., pp. 268–269.
30. François Furet underlines this point in "Burke ou la fin d'une seule histoire de l'Europe," *Le Débat* 39 (March–May 1986): 56–66.
31. Edmund Burke, "Letter to a Member of the French National Assembly in Answer to Some Objections to His Book on French Affairs," in Burke, *Works* (Boston: Little, Brown, 1839), vol. 3, p. 326.
32. Edmund Burke, *Reflections on the Revolution in France,* ed.

and intro. Conor Cruise O'Brien (Middlesex: Penguin Classics, 1986), pp. 125–126.

33. Walter Bagehot, "Letter on the New Constitution of France and the Aptitude of the French Character for National Freedom" (January 20, 1852); reproduced in Norman St. John-Stevas, *Walter Bagehot: A Study of His Life and Thought together with a Selection from His Political Writings* (Bloomington: Indiana University Press, 1959), pp. 424, 426.

34. Stefan Collini, Donald Winch, and John Burrow, *That Noble Science of Politics: A Study in Nineteenth-Century Intellectual History* (Cambridge: Cambridge University Press, 1983), p. 175. According to the preface of this fine study, the chapter on Bagehot from which I quote was written by Burrow.

35. Max Scheler, "Der Geist und die ideellen Grundlagen der Demokratien der grossen Nationen" (The spirit and the ideational bases of the democracies of the great nations), reprinted in Scheler, *Schriften zur Soziologie und Weltanschauungslehre*, 2nd ed. (Bern: Francke, 1963), *Gesammelte Werke*, vol. 6, pp. 158–186. See also the interesting comments on this essay in Adolph Lowe, *Has Freedom a Future?* (New York: Praeger, 1988), pp. 68–73.

36. Scheler, "Der Geist," pp. 182–183.

37. See Max Scheler's 1919 essay "Von zwei deutschen Krankheiten" (On two German diseases), in *Schriften zur Soziologie*, pp. 204–219. In 1923 Scheler published both papers in a collection entitled *Nation and Weltanschauung* without making any reference in his preface to the contradiction between the 1916 and 1919 essays. Scheler's wartime attitudes are discussed in Lewis Coser's introduction to *Ressentiment* (New York: Free Press of Glencoe, 1961), p. 8.

38. Friedrich A. Hayek, *The Road to Serfdom* (Chicago: University of Chicago Press, reprint ed., 1976).

39. Ibid., pp. 120–121, 122, 128.

40. See José Harris, "Einige Aspekte der britischen Sozialpolitik während des Zweiten Weltkriegs" (Some aspects of British social policy during World War II), in *Die Entstehung des Wohlfahrtsstaats in Grossbritannien und Deutschland,*

1850–1950 (The development of the welfare state in Great Britain and Germany, 1850–1950), ed. Wolfgang J. Mommsen (Stuttgart: Klett-Cotta, 1982), pp. 255–270.

41. Friedrich A. Hayek, "Freedom and the Economic System," *Contemporary Review* 153 (April 1938); reprinted in enlarged form as *Public Policy Pamphlet* 29, ed. H. D. Gideonse (Chicago: University of Chicago Press, 1938), p. 28.

42. Friedrich A. Hayek, *The Constitution of Liberty* (Chicago: University of Chicago Press, 1960), p. 256.

43. Ibid., pp. 289–290.

44. Richard Titmuss, *Essays on 'the Welfare State'* (London: Allen & Unwin, 1958), p. 34.

45. James O'Connor, *The Fiscal Crisis of the State* (New York: St. Martin's Press, 1972); the article by the same name appeared in *Socialist Revolution* 1 (January-February 1970): 12–54.

46. O'Connor, *Fiscal Crisis*, p. 6.

47. Ibid., p. 10.

48. Jürgen Habermas, *Legitimationsprobleme im Spätkapitalismus* (Frankfurt: Suhrkamp, 1973); and *Legitimation Crisis* (Boston: Beacon Press, 1975).

49. The full title is *The Crisis of Democracy: Report on the Governability of Democracies to the Trilateral Commission*, by Michel J. Crozier, Samuel P. Huntington, and Joji Watanuki (New York: New York University Press, 1975).

50. Ibid., p. 64. Emphasis in original.

51. Ibid., p. 73.

52. Nor does Huntington do so in his subsequent larger-scale work, *American Politics: The Promise of Disharmony* (Cambridge, Mass.: Harvard University Press, 1981), which elaborates on many of the themes of his essay in *The Crisis of Democracy.*

53. See Samuel P. Huntington, "Political Development and Political Decay," *World Politics* 17 (April 1965): 386–430; and *Political Order in Changing Societies* (New Haven: Yale University Press, 1968).

54. George M. Foster, *Tzintzuntzan: Mexican Peasants in a Changing World* (Boston: Little, Brown, 1967), chap. 6.
55. This topic is related to an earlier interest of mine: in *Journeys Toward Progress* (New York: Twentieth Century Fund, 1963) I analyzed various possibilities for making progress— through logrolling, shifting alliances, and the like—on two reform issues that are coming up for action more or less at the same time. See "Digression: Models of Reformmongering," in chap. 5, pp. 285–297.
56. See Huntington, *Political Order*, chap. 2; and Stein Rokkan, "Dimensions of State Formation and Nation-Building," in *The Formation of States in Western Europe*, ed. Charles Tilly (Princeton: Princeton University Press, 1975), pp. 562–600. Various alternative sequential paths are explored in Dankwart A. Rustow, *A World of Nations* (Washington, D.C.: Brookings Institution, 1967), chap. 4.
57. Albert O. Hirschman, *The Strategy of Economic Development* (New Haven: Yale University Press, 1958), pp. 118–119. The topic is treated at greater length in my 1968 article, "The Political Economy of Import-Substituting Industrialization in Latin America," reprinted in Hirschman, *A Bias for Hope: Essays on Development and Latin America* (New Haven: Yale University Press, 1971), pp. 91–96.

Five. The Three Theses Compared and Combined

1. On the background of Marx's statement, see Bruce Mazlish, "The Tragic Farce of Marx, Hegel, and Engels: A Note," *History and Theory* 11 (1972): 335–337.

Six. From Reactionary to Progressive Rhetoric

1. Leslie Stephen, "On the Choice of Representatives by Popular Constituencies," in *A Plea for Democracy*, ed. and intro. W. C. Guttsman (London: MacGibbon & Kee, 1967), pp.

72–92. I discuss this argument in *Shifting Involvements* (Princeton: Princeton University Press, 1981), pp. 115–116.

2. Helvétius, *De l'esprit* (Paris, 1758), p. 53.

3. Alexis de Tocqueville, *L'Ancien Régime et la Révolution*, 4th ed. (Paris, 1860), pp. 238–239.

4. This profusion is impressively demonstrated in Paul Bénichou, *Le temps des prophètes: Doctrines de l'âge romantique* (Paris: Gallimard, 1977).

5. Charles de Rémusat, "Burke: Sa vie et ses écrits," *Revue des deux mondes* (1853): 453. Emphasis added. This remarkable text is cited in François Furet, "Burke ou la fin d'une seule histoire de l'Europe," *Le Débat* 39 (March-May 1986): 65. Furet credits Pierre Rosanvallon with discovering it.

6. Robert C. Tucker, "The Theory of Charismatic Leadership," *Daedalus* 97 (Summer 1968): 75.

Seven. Beyond Intransigence

1. Gustave Flaubert to his niece Caroline, March 1868, in Flaubert, *Correspondance* (Paris: Conard, 1929), vol. 5, p. 367. Flaubert, commenting on the philosophical dispute over the primacy of matter or spirit, concluded: "Bref, je trouve le Matérialisme et le Spiritualisme deux impertinences égales." (In short, I find materialism and spiritualism to be two identical impertinences.) See also Jacques Derrida, "Une idée de Flaubert," in his collection *Psyché* (Paris: Galilée, 1987), pp. 305–325.

2. Bernard Crick, *In Defence of Politics*, rev. ed. (Baltimore: Penguin Books, 1964), chap. 1; and Dankwart Rustow, "Transitions to Democracy," *Comparative Politics* 2 (April 1970): 337–364.

3. This point is persuasively argued in Bernard Manin, "On Legitimacy and Political Deliberation," *Political Theory* 15 (August 1987): 338–368.

Acknowledgments

As is noted in Chapter 1, the idea for this book took shape as a result of my participation in the executive panel which the Ford Foundation put together in 1985 to advise on social welfare policies in the United States, and more specifically as I reflected on the introductory remarks of Ralf Dahrendorf at the panel's first meeting. A more remote generative influence may have been Donald McCloskey's spirited rehabilitation of rhetoric as a legitimate branch of inquiry for economists and social scientists.

In the course of writing, I received help and encouragement from a number of readers of preliminary chapter drafts. Among them I wish to mention in particular William Ewald, Joseph Frank, Luca Meldolesi, Nicoletta Stame, Fritz Stern, and Margaret Weir. Correspondence with David Bromwich, Isaac Kramnick, Jerry Muller, and Edmund Phelps helped clear up a number of points and puzzles. Pierre Andler, translator of this book into French, and Rebecca Scott gave the manuscript a final, discriminating reading. During a protracted search for the optimal title, major contributions were made by Peter Railton and Emma Rothschild.

For friends and readers to direct an author to specific texts that permit him to strengthen or adorn his argument takes altruistic behavior of a special kind. It was displayed by Walter Hinderer, Stephen Holmes, Bishop Pietro Rossano, and Quentin Skinner, as they brought to my attention highly quotable passages from works by Schiller, Maistre, Lampedusa, and Hobbes, respectively. Dennis Thompson gave valuable bibliographic advice in connection with my inquiry into the discussion around the Voting Reform Bill of 1867 in England.

Finally, it is a pleasure to acknowledge a major intellectual and personal debt to Bernard Manin. His own writings on democratic theory have been a source of continuing stimulation, and he commented generously and with his usual acumen on my evolving manuscript as we met during successive summers at Puy-Saint-Vincent in the French Alps.

Portions of this book have been presented as public lectures and at scientific meetings. A shortened version of Chapter 2 was given as a Tanner Lecture at the University of Michigan in April 1988 and subsequently at the Centre Raymond Aron in Paris and the Siemensstiftung in Munich. It was published in *The Tanner Lectures in Human Values*, vol. 10 (Salt Lake City: University of Utah Press, 1989) and, in an even shorter format, in the *Atlantic* of May 1989. At Ann Arbor, I profited from the specially commissioned critiques of John Diggins, Stephen Holmes, and Charles Tilly. Chapter 3 was presented, again in an abbreviated version, at a conference on Civil Society, held in August 1989 at Castelgandolfo under the sponsorship of the Vienna Institut für die Wissenschaften vom Menschen, and in February 1990 at a Lionel Trilling Seminar at Columbia University in New York. On the latter occasion, Stanley Hoffmann and Stephen Holmes contributed incisive comments. Chapter 4 was submitted as a discussion paper to a conference on the Philosophy of Social Choice, held in Warsaw in June 1990 and sponsored by the Polish Academy of Sciences and the American Council of Learned Societies.

From 1985 to 1989, word processing of my handwritten drafts was done with wonderful intelligence, skill, and animation by Lynda Emery. After her departure from Princeton, Lucille Allsen and Rose Marie Malarkey took over and competently saw the manuscript through its last stages. Marcia Tucker of the library of the Institute for Advanced Study provided valuable bibliographic assistance.

At Harvard University Press, which had published *Exit, Voice, and Loyalty* in 1970, Aida Donald welcomed me back with gratifying cordiality and wondrously smoothed the path from manuscript to book. Vivian Wheeler was an ideal copy editor and a most agreeable and efficient coordinator throughout the publication process. Finally, I am grateful to Gwen Frankfeldt for ably incorporating the two disputatious prophets from the Bamberg Cathedral into the cover design. This striking portrayal of intense, perhaps intransigent debate has remained imprinted in my mind ever since a visit there at age sixteen, not long before my emigration from Germany.

Index

Action, 8, 14, 152, 153. *See also* Consequences; Reaction; Side effects
Adams, John, 8
Aid to Families with Dependent Children (AFDC), 40–41, 62
Alice in Wonderland (Carroll), 44
Ampère, Jean Jacques, 47
Ancien Régime et la Révolution, L' (Tocqueville), 46, 49
Aristotle, 52
Aulard, Alphonse, 49

Bagehot, Walter, 100, 107, 108
Bentham, Jeremy, 30, 82n
Berdyaev, Nicolas, 148n
Berlin, Isaiah, 87
Beveridge Report, 111
Bias for Hope, A (Hirschman, 1971), 153n, 184n57
Bill of Rights, British, 89
Bismarck, Otto von, 132, 147
Bonald, Vicomte Louis-Gabriel-Ambroise de, 48, 165
Bright, John, 96
Burckhardt, Jacob, 21
Burke, Edmund, 35, 134n; and reaction to French Revolution, 4, 14–15, 46, 48, 161, 162, 163; and perverse effect, 12–15, 154; agreement with Adam Smith's economic views, 14; on class distinctions, 20–21; criticism of Poor Laws by, 28;

and "Cult of the British Constitution," 90; and personality foundation of democracy in France, 106–108
Burrow, John, 182n34
Butler, J. R. M., 90

Calderón de la Barca, Pedro, 154n
Candide (Voltaire), 42
Canning, George, 91
Capital (Marx), 156, 158
Carroll, Lewis, 44
"Case Against 'One Thing at a Time,' The" (Hirschman, 1990), 131n
Cité antique, La (Fustel de Coulanges, 1864), 103
Civil rights: development of, 2, 3; reaction to development of, 4, 12–13
Class distinctions: European tradition of, 20–21, 90–91, 92; and futility of universal suffrage, 51, 52, 55–56, 59, 71; in Italy, 52, 53; in socialism, 53; in oligarchies, 57, 71; and futility of welfare reform, 61–62, 63–64, 65, 68–69; in unemployment compensation, 66–67, 68–69
Claudel, Paul, 154n
Clausewitz, Carl von, 169
Club of Rome, 32
Cobban, Alfred, 13